Planning to Stay

2nd Edition

Burnout, Demoralization, Exploitation
and How to Reclaim Self-Care, Your Classroom,
and Your Life... Anyway

Jess Cleeves, MAT, LCSW

Learning Humans

Planning to Stay: Burnout, Demoralization, and Exploitation and How to Reclaim Self-Care, Your Classroom and Your Life... Anyway

2nd Edition

Published by Learning Humans Press, Salt Lake City, UT, USA. Distributed globally in English with Expanded Distribution by IngramSpark.

ISBN Paperback: 979-8-9880470-0-1
ISBN E-Book: 979-8-9880470-1-8
Library of Congress Control Number: 2023905258

 Learning Humans

For more information, please visit www.learning-humans.com.

Advanced Praise

Cleeves offers insightful and down-to-earth guidance for educators who find meaning through their work, but who are interested in ending their relationships with "psychopathic" school systems. Cleeves shows how the conditions of U.S. public education can cause burnout, demoralization, and exploitation, but she also offers guidance for those committed to finding ways to teach with integrity and joy. For teachers who want to stay but who are facing difficult conditions and unpalatable choices, this book is for you.

–**Doris Santoro**, PhD, Professor of Education, Bowdoin College, Author of *Demoralized: Why Teachers Leave The Profession They Love and How They Can Stay*

Cleeves' recent book describes a practical yet theory-based approach for realizing the joys and counteracting the challenges of being a teacher. The author shares her personal experience and stance as an educator throughout, making the book an easy and compelling read; at the same time, she presents a variety of perspectives based on current research and relevant for any educator. Compassion for the struggles many teachers face is balanced with direct and probing questions or recommendations aimed at improving teaching practices, dismantling White culture in school settings, and motivating sustained passion for exceptional work with students. At the end of each chapter, Cleeves outlines clear take-home messages and presents workbook-style checkboxes and questions that promote self-reflection and thoughtful self-care. Within the pages of Planning to Stay, beginning teachers, seasoned classroom teachers, and teacher educators alike will find immediate and relevant guidance for developing their well-being and professional joy.

–**Elisa Stone**, PhD, Program Director, CalTeach; Executive Director, Berkeley Science and Math Initiative, UC Berkeley, Berkeley, CA

Personal, insightful, relevant, and practical. This book inspires the next generation of teachers to reclaim their passion for contributing to society by naming the forces that collude, collide and contribute to teacher burnout. Wherever you are in your journey of becoming an educator or a mentor to future educators, creating and sustaining longevity requires practical sustenance. This book is it.

–**Linda Thai**, LMSW ERYT-200, Anchorage, AK

Planning to Stay offers a refreshing and honest jolt to the useless platitudes offered to teachers trying to care for themselves and their students in inhumane and unjust systems. The distinction between burnout, demoralization, and exploitation provides a way in for teachers to understand what they are feeling and to make concrete plans to reshape our relationship to the classroom and the boundaries which protect the rest of our lives.

"In order to survive my classroom, I wrote myself out of it." Starting from professional reflection on her classroom experience, Cleeves offers compassionate analysis and tough love grounded in the realities of classroom teaching, not the way we wish our schools were or the way we were told they would be in teacher preparation.

This book speaks to me—both as a former high school teacher and as a professor of education, reflecting back on my time in the classroom. If you are thinking about your future in the classroom, this book can help you feel and understand your experience. This deeply personal and insightful book is the mentor teacher you wish you had, offering reflections ranging in scale from systematic societal analysis to tips and tricks (pee breaks! email signatures!) to get you through the day.

–**Chris Proctor, PhD**, Assistant Professor of Learning Sciences, Director—University at Buffalo (SUNY) Computer Science Teacher Education Program

Planning to Stay is a timely and important book for teachers like myself, who are burned out or at risk of it (pretty much all of us!) and in need of frameworks for meaning-making and practical strategies for reconnecting with the values that drew us to the profession in the first place. Drawing on research, expertise as a mental health professional, and the grounded wisdom of a former public school teacher, Jess Cleeves offers refreshingly frank perspectives on issues that are fundamental to the day-to-day work of teachers but sorely neglected in teacher education programs and professional development. A few of these interrelated issues are teachers' mental, physical, emotional, social, and spiritual health; how boundaries can help us thrive in an exploitative education system; sustainable approaches to grading; and rehumanizing our practice and classrooms despite the structural -isms we work within. The concise explanations of these topics and the strategies that accompany them have helped me find more joy and peace in my teaching practice and life outside of work (the book reminds us there is life outside of work!), and by extension, reading Planning to Stay has benefitted my students and others dear to me.

–**Andrew Wild, PhD**, Middle School Science Teacher, Winooski, VT

For Jeannie Lythcott, who convinced Laurie Turner to mentor me, and for Laurie Turner, who accepted the challenge against her better judgment. If my practice has any shine, it's reflecting the gleam of your pure gold hearts.

Contents

Foreword

For years, I searched for a word to describe the type of success that I imagined. The world defines success in shallow ways. Money, power, and prestige are limiting and fleeting, but provide the foundation of what we imagine as success. However, wealth does not mean peace, nor does power provide joy. Teachers understand this. When we chose to teach, we rejected the world's vision of shallow success. While many consider teaching to be a noble profession, our treatment of teachers offers a fundamentally different reality. We know this; yet many of us choose to teach because we envision something well beyond standard notions of "success." I am still searching for a word to describe this goal. Planning to Stay provides more than a word for this state of mind, it gives this idea a voice.

The reality of a teacher's life is often rendered invisible by mythical movies of selfless "hero" teachers. Reality is much different. As a teacher, you need help. As a human, you need loving relationships. As an educator, you need sleep. As a person who passionately gives your time humanizing students, you need therapy. You need to laugh. You need to remember that you are supporting children. Most importantly, you need to recall that you are a person who can only give of yourself when you are operating out of the fullness of your life. The simple beauty of Planning to Stay is that it offers an honest and pragmatic guide to a life as a fulfilled teacher. It is a conversation we have behind closed doors. It is a revelation that we can be embarrassed to have with those who don't get it. However, if you are not planning to stay, you are ultimately planning to leave.

Jess Cleeves offers a new depth to the notion of teacher burnout. There is an unspoken reality in teaching. Teachers are brilliant, creative and capable, but exist in a school system and society that does not value their work. The reality that great teaching will be rendered invisible causes many to see themselves as martyrs. Teachers live parallel lives to officials or judges; you are only recognized when things go wrong. Your success lives in a state of silence. Planning to Stay offers what teacher educational programs and professional development cannot do. It shares a brutally honest understanding of the reality of schools and warns us how to maintain our lives as we are challenged with the threats of demoralization and exploitation. There is a powerful message that awaits you. The passion that brought you to the classroom must be paired with an intentional plan to keep yourself as a whole human being. Planning to Stay suggests that teachers can thrive as teachers if they humanize their students, and start by humanizing themselves.

While many discuss self-care, few describe how self-care applies to the specific role of teachers. Each day, teachers are asked to motivate and support 15–50 young people per hour. These young people arrive in our classrooms in the midst of dealing with their young lives. They are learning. While they learn, we have to engage in radical self-care in order to create a nurturing environment for our students. How can we create this environment if we neglect to create a regimen of self-care? Who is teaching us to build the cocoon of self-care for ourselves? Jess Cleeves offers a brilliant blueprint for how we can release our imperfections and accept that we, as teachers, have to grow along with our students. We have to ground ourselves in a foundation of self-care.

If you think about it, it is simple. Among the powerful revelations of this book is a message that succeeding as a teacher is not a passive act. It is hard to succeed in goals we do not set. As such, we make the job of teaching more challenging as we fail to build a plan for balance in our lives. We need a plan for mental health. We need a plan for physical health. We need a plan to fail... that is planning to stay.

If planning is the initial stage of preparing for longevity, another key is developing a deep understanding of who you are. Cleeves challenges educators to remember that we are the adults. She also commands us to remember that our students are the children. This relationship between teachers and students is one where the adult must be sure to operate in the fullness of life if they are going to be able to pour into the lives of young people. This is why many of you choose to teach and is something that, as educators, we must be vigilant to sustain. Taking an honest assessment of our own humanity stands firmly at the heart of this text. Cleeves offers divine wisdom by suggesting that every teacher remembers why we enter this business. Kids are growing. That is our joy, but not our only payment.

New goals require new words. Everyone should read this book and engage in thoughtful reflection. Start with a simple question. Am I living the life that I want to live as a teacher? Planning to Stay suggests that we should plan for a new vision of success that centers a fullness of life. Teachers should begin to re-envision a teacher's life that allows for physical, spiritual, mental, relational, and academic life.

Teachers should consider planning for a life that centers wholeness. The radical challenge to live a life that allows you to love yourself and, by default, love your students. I wish I had a word for it.

Bryan A. Brown, PhD
Professor, Science Education
Stanford University

COVID-19/CRT Statement

"It is inconceivable that a sovereign people should continue, as we do so abjectly, to say 'I can't do anything about it. It's the Government.' The government is the creation of the people. It is responsible to the people. And the people are responsible for it."
— James Baldwin —

As of the release date of this second edition, 1145 days have passed since March 13, 2020. The heartbreak and loss contained by those 1145 days are equivalent to many lifetimes' worth. To those of you who have generally returned to "life as usual," the residue of the pandemic may still be gumming up the works of your teaching practice. To those of you for whom grief is a constant companion, for whom no amount of time will completely dull the pain, for those who lost loved ones, relationships, stability, and faith during this jagged few years, though it will never be consolation, I mourn with you.

I can't help but feel foolish as I look back at the start of the pandemic. For a few brief moments before the rolling devastation set in, I had hope. Now I understand now naïve it was, but I did have hope, initially. I had a foolish hope that, by facilitating their childrens' learning from home, parents would be overwhelmed by appreciation and gratitude for teachers. On realizing how integral schools were to the functioning of both individual families and the global economy, I expected a cascade of educator-supporting initiatives: funding for educator homeownership and loan forgiveness programs, legislation to increase teacher pay and decrease class sizes, even less gate-keepy academic recognition for educators' advanced training, experience, and contributions. I hoped for a wave of curious, motivated volunteerism from community members who benefit, de-facto, from the work that teachers do. Heck, I even hoped for empathy.

I was wrong.

I was so very wrong, and in so many ways. As I watched wealthy White parents team up with their neighbors to self-fund learning pods, I was certain that community organizations would support poor parents of color to stay home and facilitate similar neighborhood groups. There was not. I was confident that parents would be understanding as they inquired about confusion over a unit that their child's teacher had barely built and got online at 2 a.m. that same morning. I was incorrect. In my work supporting administrators, I heard the same thing again and again: "The district says we're on our own." In my work with educators, I heard a similar refrain: "My admin says I'm on my own."

Our collective regard for public education was revealed at every stage of this multi-stage pandemic. At every stage, the conclusions were consistent: regard for educators is neutral-to-disparaging, and no one is coming.

Except teachers. Teachers came. Teachers *showed up*.

Teachers showed up for their students. Teachers prioritized learning new platforms over sleeping. Teachers drove materials to students' homes when they were uncertain where they would find their own basic supplies for daily life. Teachers made phone calls to speak with families about their student's needs though they could barely force words through their own anxiety. Teachers greeted students with unfailing joy through their own unrelenting grief. Teachers dragged themselves out of bed, splashed cold water on their faces (still puffy from crying), and turned on that damn camera.

Granted, not all of them. The last three years have led to an unprecedented and wholly understandable exodus, with teachers leaving the classroom at record rates. To those who left, we say "Congratulations!" Better for someone to have left the profession than stay in it and expose students to their hurt and frustration. For those of you whose own children were harmed by under-resourced and under-supported teachers, I don't mean to invalidate that very real harm, and I'm so sorry. For those of you who stayed in the classroom but didn't want to, I am sorry for how terrible that likely feels.

I was one of those who left. I changed careers entirely in January 2021. I made this major decision as the institution that employed me responded to pandemic demands by continually prioritizing profit over people and leadership's comfort over the needs of the students we served. I left with sadness, with fear, and with resolve.

It was a mournful experience to face spring 2021 as my first semester without students in nearly two decades. I feared that the moment I stepped out of the classroom, I would lose all street cred with in-class-room teachers (but that had already happened when I left K-12 for the university classroom; I survived, and I found that I was, indeed, still able to support educators). My resolve was two-fold: I wanted to build a livelihood that aligned with my values, and I hoped to provide teachers with meaningful support.

When I left academia, some colleagues cut me off out of judgment for my decision. Many remained in community with me. Through ongoing personal, professional, and public conversations in this community, it is evident that many more teachers are still considering leaving. They don't stay in their current classrooms out of an overwhelming sense of duty, but because they don't know what else to do. Many teachers stay because they feel trapped, which feels like disempowerment stacked on top of disempowerment.

As of today, it's been 1072 days since George Floyd was murdered. From an educator's perspective, the pandemic was tough, but it didn't feel very personal. In contrast, the way the nation's brush with what could have been a racial reckoning funneled into the CRT debate—and the policy changes that debate inspired—that was personal. Around the nation, these policy changes codified permission for the micro-management of teachers' curricular decisions and created bureaucratic busy work as a smokescreen for what Dr. LaGarrett King refers to as "the opposition to the teaching of history."

When sitting down to write this book, I debated including information about structural oppression. I wasn't sure the struggling teacher would find such a structural view useful. As the structural oppression of the teaching profession has been the final straw that has driven so many out of the classroom, I understand now that including such an analysis was absolutely necessary. Many teachers may not have been explicitly motivated by social justice values at the start of their career, but as they were asked to work in the service of social injustice, many came to understand that social justice is inexorably linked with teaching in public schools. We don't need to explicitly discuss politics for this to matter; many teachers may not yet understand the relationship between their own stress and structural oppression. I hope that this book will begin that exploration for those new to the idea.

The way that teachers continue to be treated in the wake of a global pandemic and a democracy-shaking racial reckoning is appalling. Unconscionable. Inexcusable. As work in trauma recovery demonstrates, however, it's possible for something to happen that is not okay, but for the victim to claim ways to be okay anyway. Victimization, in some limited respects, is a two-way street; just because educators have been victimized doesn't mean that teachers must automatically accept identities as victims. No one can take our dignity without our permission.

Education has a long history of blaming the victim. Both students and educators are frequently individually blamed for systemic failure. Such victim blaming is a key component of perpetuating this stable-but-harmful system. Let's be abundantly clear here: teachers can't self-care their way out of systemic abuse. And no teacher has to accept an identity of powerless victim.

It's been three years since we quarantined. If any sweeping positive reforms were going to happen at a policy level, they would have happened already. As we admit that the people who are most capable of improving public schools are the least likely to lead that change, we are invited to something different. Rather than martyring ourselves to an unchanging system, we are invited to acknowledge that the values motivating the current system are, at their core, different from those which drew us to the profession. We are invited to acknowledge that, upon walking into a classroom, we are walking into a dishonest space. We are walking into a space obscured by a veneer of good will. We now deeply understand that it is a space willing to inflict harm. Indeed, we know for certain that it will do us harm, if we allow it. And so each and every educator must protect themselves. Not because education is hopeless, but because educators themselves are the only hope.

Based on the way our institutions have reacted to the last two years of sociocultural strain, it has become abundantly clear that if public education is going to change, it will be because the people who make it all happen— the educators themselves—both demand and design that change. This is annoyingly inconvenient. It is unfair. It is also true.

It is challenging to negotiate from a position of strength while also claiming an identity as a victim. Victimized teachers, there is possibility here; if you wish to stay in teaching because of your own convictions, you can. It is unlikely that staying, however, will be easy. Staying will likely require a significant shift in perspective. Staying may well require that you shore yourself up, that you fortify your convictions against the active battlefield that is the profession. Staying might even be supported by the decision to methodically, committedly, and strategically begin to organize for the broad-scale change that your hard-earned wisdom knows is necessary. That effort is a burden. It is unpaid. No one will give you credit towards your salary schedule for having done it. The only acknowledgement you'll likely get for that kind of system-shifting work will likely be from your own sense of having participated in something that truly matters.

You get to leave if you want to. Truly. Unequivocally. If you are staying because you feel trapped, may you have the energy, space, and creativity necessary to find a situation that works for you, or at least an exit strategy that gives you hope. May you be free to go, if that's what you need. Please consider, however, that instead of a reactive, sunglasses-on, slow-motion walk away from the explosion behind you, perhaps you may leave the classroom without abandoning your commitment to the work. Perhaps you may leave the classroom to find a home in transformational policy work, to school board membership, to serve as an elected official. In-classroom educators need, and deserve, all of the support they can get, and there is no one better to advocate for educators than someone who knows, intimately, what it's like to be one.

Goodness knows, if you want to stay, that's okay, too. It's possible that, even given all that the last three years have revealed, your heart is still pulled towards the classroom by an abiding sense of purpose. If you want to stay because you know in your core that this is the work that you want to do, then trust that feeling. Honor that feeling, and honor it well. May you support yourself to be as strong and as well-protected as possible towards being as effective as possible, both for your students and for how you know schools could be. Hopefully this book can support your essential work in your choice to stay, as that is its intention. After all, the only way schools will go from what they are to what they could be is if a whole lot of us put in a whole lot of strategic, dedicated work from whatever corner of the system we can reach.

It's true, no one is coming.

It's a good thing you are there.

~~Introduction~~ Permission Slip

"If you don't like something, change it.
If you can't change it, change your attitude."
— Maya Angelou —

Instead of an Introduction, I offer this Permission Slip to any educators reading this book. I invite you to use this book, not just read it. Wherever you are on your journey with teaching—ready to leave the profession today, or afraid you'll be forced to give up some day because of the toll teaching takes—this book can help. Particularly if you use it however you want to.

Many books for teachers are either about classroom strategies for managing students, or about how to fix schools by describing how they should work in the future. This book is neither of those. This book acknowledges that you are teaching in a less-than-ideal system today, and that many things beyond pedagogical strategies impact your life as an educator. It also acknowledges that you can deploy the best strategies, but if you do so while poorly regulated due to unmanaged stress, you can still harm your students. If you are feeling burned out, demoralized, or exploited, it is not your fault. This book will not simply tell you to think more positively or take more bubble baths. It's both a manual from which you can create your plan to stay, and an exploration of the systemic reasons behind why many have found it increasingly challenging to do so.

To effectively address a problem, we must understand it. In the first section, this book examines the subtle, pervasive, under-acknowledged reasons that teaching is hard (hint: it's not just you). Then, having named those underlying reasons, the second half of the book offers specific ways to shift your expectations, focus, goals, and actions in order to reclaim your joy in spite of structural challenges.

Your experience as an educator is your own, and only you can create your path back to passion and meaning. My hope, however, is that this book will support you to do just that. With more information and straightforward tools and processes to support you, you can create your plan to stay. You just have to give yourself permission to do so.

This form authorizes _You_ , a fully autonomous and empowered educator and expert in your own instructional context and personal needs, to read this book however _You_ want to.

If this is true for you	Consider starting here
I'm ready to quit tomorrow	Chapter 5 - Self-care for survival
I need strategies ASAP	Chapter 7 - Whole year Chapter 8 - Lesson plans Chapter 9 - Grading
I'm exhausted, but I can't say "no"	Chapter 4 - You CAN set boundaries!
I'm starting to resent my students	Chapter 6 - "Helping" can accidentally hurt
I don't know what's wrong with me/ I like to start with definitions	Chapter 2 – Definitions and diagnosis
Teaching is different than expected	Chapter 6 - We teach in the real world Chapter 10 - Teaching is harder than advertised
I complain a lot because I don't know what else to do	Chapter 3 - Learn how to process effectively
I put others before myself	Chapter 1 - You can (and must) change your life
My students' experiences are my primary concern	Chapter 11 – Your state impacts your classroom
Big change is overwhelming	Chapter 10 - Small changes, big impact
I hate planning/I love planning, but forget to eat	Chapter 12 - Plan for your whole real life
I'm too tired to read, but need some hope	Chapters end with **"Too Long; Didn't Read"** summaries of ideas and strategies

While the list above is a guide to possible approaches, the reader of this book is in no way constrained, and may change approaches at any time.

Signature: _Your Innate Sense of What's Best for You_   Date: _Whenever It's Useful_

Section 1

Who, What, and Why

Chapter 1

Your Time Is All You Have

In which we explore your mortality and the possibility that you deserve to live in a manner that allows you to die without regret.

"I'd rather wear out than rust out."

— Dolly Parton —

Your Classroom Will Take Everything. If You Let It.

I know because I let it.

This is a book about how to stay in the classroom written by someone who left. Because of the culture of loyalty teaching demands, this fact may turn many educators away from these pages automatically. After all, what could I possibly know? I'm a quitter.

It's true, I quit teaching. I didn't, however, quit learning. After my decade in the classroom took my health, my partnership, and my happiness, I spent five years working with teachers who needed the kind of support I could have used. I went back to school and used my graduate studies in social work to understand what happened to me, and what is happening for so many teachers. This book summarizes many of the things I've learned about the key ideas and practices that have allowed educators to reclaim their classrooms and their lives.

It's true, at one point, I did let my classroom take everything. I know what that feels like. I also know what it feels like to find balance, purpose, and joy in work—even during the school year. In my work supporting teachers, so many were able to find their way to balance, reclamation, and joy that I felt compelled to offer you the same tools, the same vision, the same feeling. If you're open to hearing from a quitter, that is...

Sadly, you're not alone. Educators around the country have discovered the insatiability of the gig; if you allow it, your classroom will take every waking second. Even if you're not physically at school nor actively working, your constant preoccupation can claim every moment of your life.

Your classroom can stand between you and the people in your life, and even between you and your life itself. The demand has the potential to be never-ending; you could constantly strive to perfect another lesson, and, once it's been perfected, you could continuously better-customize it for this year's students, this particular period's students, students as distinct individuals. There will never be a time when zero students would benefit from another hour of one-on-one support, another call to a family member, another reminder about the quiz Friday, and the free dental clinic appointment sign-up Monday.

What's great is that, if you're like most teachers, you've never received specific, targeted instruction on how to design your approach to maximize your joy-rich efficacy while minimizing the tasks that steal your soul. Why is that great? It's great because it means that you may think the long march to classroom soul-sacrifice is inevitable. Let's correct that perception here and now: the long march to classroom soul-sacrifice is not inevitable. This is great news because you're about to learn how honoring yourself will support your commitment to being an excellent teacher—as a part of living an excellent life, which also happens to include teaching.

The tasks that devour teachers' time are usually not the tasks that make teaching meaningful.

Teachers can—and must—take control of their time in order to both live their values and value their lives. You can do this by owning your time. This book will guide you to build a comprehensive approach to planning which merges:
- Your professional obligations
- Targeted self-care for excellence and joy in classroom and life
- Calendaring (a verb) to enact the life you wish to cultivate
- By-the-minute lesson planning to ensure that the values that brought you to the profession are evident in your classroom interactions

By building and enacting these skills, you can protect:
- Your peace and happiness
- Your professional power
- Your relationships (both in your personal life and with students)
- Your going-to-die-one-day integrity

It will take some work. But that's okay. We already know you're pretty good at that. ;)

On Your Way Out Already?

If you are reading this as you actively consider leaving, please consider one possibility (via morbid metaphor) before you go; in emergency medicine, someone who appears to have perished due to hypothermia can't be declared deceased until they are "warm and dead." In hypothermia, the body's processes slow down so much that people can appear dead, be closed in a body bag, and then sit upright hours later, bewildered and very much alive, because their core temperature was allowed to increase slowly and safely.

If you can bear it, consider resisting the urge to quit when you're cold; don't quit in the heart of your pain, frustration, sadness, exhaustion, and hopelessness. If your health, family, and sanity can bear it, consider warming up first. Explore the approaches and complete the exercises in this book, perhaps for as little as one more month of active teaching. I hope that having done so, you'll be able to make the most empowered, information-rich decision possible, based on the realization that you may be able to not just tolerate, but become deeply fulfilled again by your practice.

From a calm, centered place, it may feel not only possible, but powerful and exciting to plan to stay.

Teachers are Meaning-Seekers

This book is about time. Out of respect for yours, let's get right to the point; you are going to die.

This is the only thing I know about you with absolute certainty. Because you're an educator, I have a few other guesses about who you are and what's important to you. I'll be wrong about many of them. Still, we'll build enough flexibility into the strategies and frameworks you're about to explore that, when I inevitably get it wrong, you'll still be able to be yourself within them in spite of the specific examples I offer.

You know what's less flexible? Death. It is coming for every one of us. Perhaps tomorrow, ideally quite a-ways down the road. But unfailingly, absolutely, and inevitably.

Your time is all you have. And you have less of it now than you did when you started reading the previous paragraph. Owning your mortality is profoundly motivating. Once mortality stops feeling scary (or if it never does), you can switch from ignoring to owning your mortality.

Because you've chosen to dedicate your time to your students (at least some of it—we'll get to "how much" later on), I can assume that you've already made some decisions about the values shaping your life. Making lots of money might be less important to you than a reliable—though slimmer—paycheck. Connecting and sharing with students may be more important to you than winning arguments, collecting awards, or advancing up a steep professional hierarchy. Of the hundreds of teachers I've worked with, the vast majority are deeply committed to and motivated by a meaningful work life. In the very decision to become educators, they have already made a decisive move towards a life that matters.

Something starts to happen to us in classrooms, though. The classroom takes our time by the wrist and twists. We're educators—we're strong, resilient, and resourceful, so we keep smiling and start to frantically try to figure it out internally. We think if we work harder, the grip will loosen. Goodness knows it's too shameful to cry "uncle," to admit it's too much.

Sometimes the rift between the values that drew us to the gig and the ways we're asked to behave cleaves open like a tectonic event; our job changes overnight as our institution is converted to a "turn-around" school with mandatory, daily, 20-minute faculty "pep talks" at 7 a.m., where students are tested with such regularity that we volunteer to build afterschool programming just to create space in which students aren't being harmed by every part of school—even as we work as district employees enacting the very harm our own volunteerism strives to counteract.

Sometimes the hijacking of our time starts less noticeably; we stay late once to get ahead on grading, we sacrifice a weekend to figure out why the district's wifi won't work with our laptop, we drive an assignment to a house three counties away because we know that that kid didn't pick up their homework because Child Protective Services got involved. Then we turn around five years later and realize there has not been one single weeknight we've arrived home before 7 p.m. We've built the expectation in our students' caregivers that our above-and-beyond mentality is the standard. We can't sleep nor socialize gracefully for thinking about the ungraded work, the approaching unplanned unit. We also (hopefully) realize that we've missed birthdays and anniversaries and parties and trips with people we love because they happen to fall within the academic calendar.

Our bodies ache. We gain weight.[1] We lose touch with friends. We are grouchy and unavailable to our own families. We aren't who we want to be, neither in our classrooms nor in our lives.

If we aren't careful, the values, activities, and tasks that brought us to the profession and bring us joy within it get pushed out by the tasks we feel obligated, compelled, tricked and manipulated into—if we even notice that we've been tricked, that this isn't what we signed up for, that this isn't how we want to teach. Heck, this isn't how we want to live.

We can learn a lot about how to live from the dying. Bronnie Ware, a palliative care nurse, compiled trends in the regrets that people expressed as she supported their final days.[2] The most frequently expressed regrets she heard from her patients:

- I wish I had the courage to live a life true to myself, not the life others expected of me.
- I wish I hadn't worked so hard.
- I wish I had the courage to express my feelings.
- I wish I had stayed in touch with my friends.
- I wish I had let myself be happier.

While this list is precious for its simplicity and the simple directives we can take from it, it's also a sneaky trick for teachers. If we're not careful, we can glance at this list and, on the surface, feel like we're slaying the no-death-bed-regrets game. We can fool ourselves into thinking that our very choice of profession in itself will save us from experiencing the regrets this list

---

[1] I note rapid weight gain as a symptom of uncontrolled stress. Body fat is culturally demonized, but is not a health problem on its own. Fat can be present in people who exercise regularly and eat plant-rich diets:

Bacon, L. (2010). Health at every size: The surprising truth about your weight. BenBella Books, Inc.

Campos, P. F. (2004). The obesity myth: Why America's obsession with weight is hazardous to your health. Penguin.

Gordon, A. (2023). "You Just Need to Lose Weight": And 19 Other Myths About Fat People. Beacon Press.

[2] Ware, B. (2012). The top five regrets of the dying: A life transformed by the dearly departing. Hay House, Inc.

frames. If we're good at this self-deception, we could end up enacting the precise opposite of the list.

If we're going to last in the classroom with integrity, joy, and connection to our life's purpose, the first step to using this list as an instruction manual is to examine our current life with unflinching honesty.

I Wish I Had Lived a Life True to Myself, Not the Life Others Expected of Me.

For those of us who were pushed to pursue status-rich professions like law and medicine, the simple act of choosing to teach may feel like a permanent, flying leap into "living a life true to myself." The relief of having escaped a Big Regret may be tempered when we think about the hours (years?) we've spent grading quizzes that students promptly place in the nearest recycling bin. I'd wager that scripted curricula and district-mandated benchmarks weren't the first things that came to your mind when considering what a life lived true to yourself would look like. When evaluating this list in comparison to your life, consider comparing it to how your work as an educator *actually* looks instead of how you thought it would or how you wish it did.

Living a life true to ourselves first requires that we know who we are. Knowing who we are is a process, not product. We are constantly learning and growing, and, therefore, we must be constantly open to learning about who we are now. Who you were when you started your teacher prep journey is different from who you are now. The experiences you've had, the students and colleagues you've been influenced by, the way your local and global landscapes have moved and changed—all of these will impact who you are constantly becoming. Having the courage to live a life true to ourselves requires a primacy, a prioritization, in how we approach our work because it demands that we perpetually both know and inquire about who we are.

If we lull ourselves into complacency regarding this first potential regret, which is what happens if we consider this box checked simply because of our choice to teach, we also lull ourselves out of sensitivity to how the expectations of others impact our practices. My guess is that many of the people Ms. Ware interviewed thought about their parents and mentors when they mourn for the way they caved to others' expectations. For educators, the "others" who claim a right to have expectations about our behavior are much more numerous. Our "others" include the federal government, the state, our district, our school, our administrators, and all of the families we serve. All of these parties have expectations of teachers. Because of this tremendous expectational pressure, if we aren't firmly anchored to who we are, if we haven't built sustaining practices to constantly tighten the knot which binds us to a life lived true to ourselves, it's too easy to get swept away by that sea of expectation.

I Wish I Hadn't Worked So Hard.

Many of us truly do love what we do; high-fiving students as they enter our rooms for after-school homework help feels good, and color-coding our grading scheme offers a perverse pleasure. Because components of the job are truly rewarding, we don't notice when we're working too hard.

That's how addiction works, though, isn't it?

To our brains, there is little difference between the shot of feel-good chemicals we get from feeling accomplished versus the rush of neurotransmitters that comes with a snort of cocaine. The only reason this is a problem is because our world doesn't act like it's a problem. If we stayed late, bailed on plans, and allowed our health to deteriorate because we were sitting at our desks snorting coke, we would face the admonishment, disappointment, and intervention of our friends, family, and community. Rather, our perverse addiction is tolerated. It's tolerated because we convince ourselves that it's for The Greater Good, and our culture not only allows but benefits significantly from this distortion.

A line that clinical professionals haven't yet been able to draw very clearly is where working hard crosses into workaholism. Just like other forms of addiction, each individual must themselves agree with a diagnosis based on whether they think a behavior is both compulsive and negatively impacting their lives. Put that way, workaholism seems like a really simple idea.

Workaholism is more complex than simply staying at work too late. Workaholism can show up in how compelled we feel to start a project, complete a project, or even how much we avoid a project. Understanding these features may help you to figure out if you are closer to workaholic ways of being than you might think:

Clinical researcher Professor Bryan Robinson identifies two axes for workaholics: work initiation and work completion. He associates the behavior of procrastination with both "Savoring Workaholics" (those with low work initiation, low work completion, or both) and "Attention-Deficit Workaholics" (those with high work initiation and low work completion), in contrast to "Bulimic" and "Relentless" workaholics—both of whom have high work completion.[3]

Think you're not a workaholic because of how much time you spend putting off work, full of dread? Based on Dr. Robinson's framework, your procrastination counts as working too hard; it's still time that your physical, mental, and emotional energy are consumed by work, and you're not absent for the rest of your life. Your family, your home, your body—none of them care why you aren't attending to them. They simply know that you aren't.

You are allowed to work hard. Working hard can, indeed, enrich our lives. As the deathbed regret states, however, you're not allowed to work so hard that you forfeit your life. Finding that line is challenging; requires ongoing evaluation, and, most importantly, is possible.

I Wish I Had the Courage to Express My Feelings.

Many of us express feelings frequently and freely—but only to our captive, probably-shouldn't-hear-that students. Better outlets for our emotions are the people closest to us who are craving connection or the humans in powerful positions who can respond to our professional frustrations with action.

Expressing adult emotion to our students unfairly puts them in a caretaking role, even if we're doing it in the spirit of transparency and connection. Putting our students in the position of attending to our emotions is unhelpful at best, and dangerous at worst. Ideally, teachers would all be provided high-quality mental health care to have a supportive, therapeutic outlet for their real, important, influential emotions. Unfortunately, many therapists don't get teaching's unique challenges, so many teachers who seek such support on their own can feel dismissed, unseen and under-supported by their clinicians. Similarly, our faith communities and peers who work in other sectors may not grasp the depth of connection between who we are and what we do. All of this can add up to emotions that have nowhere to go, so are aimed inappropriately at our students.

You've heard of the phrase "hurt people hurt people"? Think of a time

---

[3] Robinson, B. E. (2000). A typology of workaholics with implications for counselors. Journal of Addictions & Offender Counseling, 21(1), 34-48.

you spoke sharply to a student, raised your voice, reacted in a manner that you're not proud of when a class was behaving differently than you'd hoped. How many of those times were those feelings actually about that one, single, specific situation or student vs. being about that situation or student as informed by the layers of stress, unexamined internal dialogue, and unexpressed feelings you had about your worth, your abilities, your sense of well-being and place in the world feeling somehow threatened?

By protecting spaces and relationships in our lives for our own emotional processing, we protect our students from our worst days. We know they won't remember much from our classes, but we are damn sure we don't want the one thing they remember to be that time we made them feel small because our big feelings had nowhere else to go.

I Wish I Had Stayed in Touch with My Friends.

Some of our colleagues feel like friends. So do our students, particularly if we start to put the unfair burden of supporting our emotional well-being on them as we drift further and further from our real-life friends who may not understand the professional pressures we feel.

It's okay if our only friends are our colleagues as long as those friends are also unflinchingly supportive, don't permit unproductive negative "venting" (aka complaining), are in no way in competition with us for material or social resources in our school, district, and state, and have the capacity to be available when we really need them. As you know, during the school year, it's tough for any educator to meet these criteria.

Friendships, especially in adulthood, require both consistent tending and clear agreements about the depth and level of commitment we will share. In some ways, your colleagues are primed to meet those needs for you. In many other ways, the structure of teaching itself stacks the deck against your best friends being educators. Do you need to change your friend roster? Not necessarily. You get to think about what you need, what you want, and what you'd like to do about both. And there's no rush.

It's okay if we don't spend any time with educators in our private lives. This configuration, however, also has its challenges. If your friends can celebrate that being a teacher is an essential, core component of your identity without allowing it to be your entire identity, keep 'em! If you feel like you need to make yourself small, apologize for your boundaries, or feel constantly pressured or like you're disappointing them, you may want to reassess those friendships.

Again, no rush, no pressure. And... it's worth considering.

Finally, having either 100% teacher friends or 100% other-sector friends is far better than having very few adult friendships and expecting students to fulfill your relationship needs. When we expect to matter as much to students as they reciprocally matter to us, we are crossing essential boundaries as adults in mentorship roles; the consequences for students can range from "bummer" to devastating. The devastating side of that scale of student experiences overlaps with educator behavior that is both wildly inappropriate and illegal. If we are not managing the health of our out-of-school relationships, our in-school relationships are at risk of becoming extremely unhealthy. And harmful.

Think this isn't a problem? Sexual contact between educators and students is increasing at every grade level.[4] If a connection-starved practitioner isn't able to manage their desire to text a student, allow physical contact, or even teach a student about what disclosures are better shared with a school social worker or therapist, the same reward circuitry in our brains can take over relationship management, just as it can with workaholism. We can find ourselves justifying unnecessarily and harmfully close "friendships" with the students in our care.

It is our job for us to be there for our students as kind, unflinching adults who negotiate the ups and downs of their developmental adventures with unconditional positive regard, an unwavering belief in their capacities to learn, grow, and be okay, and an abiding commitment to maintaining the boundaries that keep them whole and safe. If we are counting on our students for any relationship beyond us being there for them within the scope of our training, we are unequivocally doing it wrong.

Of course, being there for our students as appropriate and capable mentors while needing nothing from them in return is both a noble and gigantic ask. It's not easy to need nothing from other humans you care about. The only way to do it, however, is to truly need nothing from them.

---

[4] Grant, B. J. (2018). A Case Study of K-12 School Employee Sexual Misconduct: Lessons Learned from Title IX Policy Implementation, United States, 1984-2014.

Because you do need social support, it's your obligation to maintain rich, meaningful relationships outside of the classroom. If you won't do it for yourself, understand that you need to do it for your students.

I Wish I Had Let Myself Be Happier.

This last one—happiness—might be the trickiest. The key here is the "let myself." What would happen if we let ourselves feel more happiness? Choosing to teach in our culture means that educators trade some real, concrete benefits like social status and the ability to eat out whenever we want for the work that fulfills us. Unfortunately, we're the ones who tend to extend the formula.

We manage to take it from "teaching isn't as nice as other gigs" to "we don't deserve nice things."

Just because teaching is hard doesn't mean we're better teachers by making it feel harder. Self-denial of joy presents in many ways but very often with a feeling of guilt that overshadows anything that starts to feel good. We see this when we need to fill our summers with work tasks in order to respond to the internalized critique that we can't suffer because we get summers off. We see this when we're ready for class tomorrow, but we skip softball league to stay in the classroom until 6pm to prep for next week because softball happens every week, so we can just catch it next Wednesday.

Sometimes we are so ashamed of the fact that parts of our extremely difficult job do bring us joy and have very real perks that we grab that joy and jiu jitsu kick-flip it to the ground before anyone can detect that we are both capable and deserving of happiness. We do this when we reject praise from colleagues, when we can't celebrate wins with students, when we switch to listing everything that went wrong in a lesson before we name one single component that went right. Sometimes we reject joy simply due to our own insecurity. Sometimes, it's impossible to consider that, even if there's always more work to do, we are not more worthy nor more valuable nor more essential for having done it.

This is bad news, both because of how regularly and how completely it happens. We start to believe that our misery is an essential part of an effective teaching practice. The good news? This bologna is self-imposed! We get to fix it. We get to learn, allow, embrace, and cultivate happiness.

We get to enjoy our work.

Too Long; Didn't Read
Chapter 1:
Your Time Is All You Have

Ideas

According to the top 5 regrets of the dying, teachers are at unique risk of building deathbed regrets:

- **I wish I had the courage to live a life true to myself, not the life others expected of me.** Educators are at risk of this regret because we feel accountable to expectations from ourselves, our students, and our families, as well as at the school, district, state, and federal levels.
- **I wish I hadn't worked so hard.** Working too hard steals time from the rest of our lives, regardless of how worthy the cause.
- **I wish I had the courage to express my feelings.** Teachers might express their feelings well, but only sometimes to the right audiences. We are often impoverished in adult relationships, so we are prone to both ineffectual venting that doesn't lead to meaningful change and inappropriately leaning on our students to field our emotional needs.
- **I wish I had stayed in touch with my friends.** Adult friendships are challenging to maintain for everyone, but the pressures of teaching make us particularly vulnerable to losing track of the relationships we value the most.
- **I wish I had let myself be happier.** The martyr model of teaching has trained us to go without pleasure for so long that we can cultivate guilt about feeling happy even during our hard-earned free time. Teachers deserve as much access to experiencing happiness as anyone.

Strategies

- Acknowledge your risk of dying with regret.
- Be open to the possibility that you have the power to change your experience in a way that will be better for your students, your loved ones, and most importantly, yourself.

Chapter 2

Burnout vs. Demoralization vs. Exploitation

In which we categorize the ways in which good teachers are harmed by the profession and how good teachers can harm the profession, their students, and themselves. We also determine if you are burned out, demoralized, exploited, or some combination of all three.

"It's not the load that breaks you down;
it's the way you carry it."
— Lena Horne —

Defining the Experience

The distinction I'm about to present between burnout, demoralization, and exploitation is not universally agreed upon. Some people build careers researching burnout but define it more like how I define demoralization. Fewer people have heard of demoralization in an educational setting, as the idea is much more popular in nursing scholarship (where it's referred to as "moral injury"). Both nursing and education depend upon exploiting the dispositions and commitments of service-motivated practitioners, so neither mentions exploitation much at all. I have no interest in picking fights with the academics building their CVs on these terms. Rather, these definitions are purely for your purposes—a framework to help you start to name what you may be experiencing toward building your own strategic interventions.

A mom was the first person to ask me if I was burned out. Her daughter was a 9th grader in my freshman biology class. Mom had requested a meeting because, per school policy, I had confiscated her daughter's phone after her daughter texted in class. Though this was the first time someone asked me if I was "burned out," I understood both what the phrase was supposed to mean and that it wasn't all-encompassing enough to capture how educators can fall out of love with—and be harmed by—the profession. We'll use this "phone incident," a bummer interaction I had with a student and parent, as a case study to explore the difference between burnout, demoralization, and exploitation. As I tell it, I'll also note some mistakes I made in case my blunders can prevent a rookie educator from doing the same. Decision point #1: I chose to call during my "lunch," a distracting and distracted time. The student had been texting during a dissection and had exhausted a three-strikes approach (phone out and in-use about non-school stuff 3 times), so she was behind on the lab. Also in the room: students staying to finish dissections, students making up missing assignments, and some of the 46 students in the recently-adjourned class were taking a while to pack up and head out. The room was full and loud.

"Hi, Ms. Mom, I'm calling to let you know that your daughter was using her phone during class. It's been confiscated per school policy, and you can pick it up from the front office whenever you'd like." This was a tiny lie, as the phone was not yet physically in the office—I needed to figure out how to get it to the 1st floor office from the 4th floor while young people with scalpels were still in my classroom.

"Oh, I'm sure you're mistaken. My daughter is an excellent student. She would never text during class."

"Okay," I replied as four students lined up for me to sign their tracking sheets for discipline contracts for other teachers, sports, their probation officers... "But she did, and per school policy, it will be waiting for you at the office." Face. Palm. This was the precise point at which I agreed to Mom's stance that we would be adversaries. That was Decision Point #2. But, wait! There's more...

"So am I understanding that, because there's been a misunderstanding between you and my daughter, I now need to interrupt my workday to come and get the phone that she has never, not one single time, used during class, and that she has on her at all times *for safety reasons*?" No doubt this example sticks in my mind because of the masterful range of argumentative maneuvers Mom deployed in such a short conversation.

"Ma'am," Ouch! Decision point #3. I should have led with her dang name. "Your daughter had her phone out during a lab that involved serious safety concerns. There wasn't a misunderstanding; the expectation is clear and outlined in the disclosure you signed at the start of the year. I am doing my best to support my 280 students to stay focused and learning this term. I'm grateful for your help. I will now return to the classroom of students I have committed to helping during my lunch period. The phone will be waiting for you in the office." Click.

Did you catch them all? Here are a few more decision points for analysis:

4. Reinforced adversarial stance by correcting Mom's language.
5. Reminded Mom that she agreed to the policy she was fighting, which was received as attacking her competency/good-mom-ness.
6. I lied about being grateful for her help. I was actually annoyed as hell that she wasn't helping me at all, which she could probably hear pretty clearly through my clenched-jaw enunciation.
7. In stating how many students I was attempting to support, I diluted the specialness of her daughter as one of my students (in her eyes). I martyred myself, implying I couldn't handle teaching.
8. I admitted I was working during lunch, confirming the martyr model (evidence for her that I was already willing to give up what I need to support the needs of others; if helicopter moms are sharks, information like this is like blood in the water).
9. I hung up. On her. Hung up the whole damn phone. Yes, yes I did. Not 20 minutes later, with only slightly less chaos in the classroom, the Assistant Principal came in and asked if he could speak with me. Of course, he did.

That afternoon, when, per Mom's request, I met with Mom and daughter, (read: Mom's demand to the Assistant Principal, whom she found time to call immediately in the middle of her workday which was otherwise totally unacceptable to interrupt), she seethed.

"Aren't you here to support students?" she asked. "How long have you been teaching? Is that what you think support looks like? Are you *burned out* or something?" Her eyes gleamed with a spark of pleasure when she said it, like she had gotcha-ed me. And it worked—it landed like an accusation, like it was the meanest thing she could have said.

Something inside of me needed to immediately reject the possibility that I had burned out. Because to burn out is to fail. To be a failure. To personally lack the fortitude, creativity, and aptitude to flourish as an educator. While anyone might deny such a painful charge even if it was true,

I also somehow knew that it wasn't. I hadn't burned out. But I wasn't okay.

It was a ridiculous, annoying interaction that I handled badly. If I had known more about myself, particularly how I was impacted by burnout, demoralization, and exploitation, I certainly would have had more of my better self available in the interaction. Perhaps I could have prevented the whole thing entirely.

Heck. Perhaps I would still be a teacher.

Teaching Can Be Oppressive

Oppression is "the unjust or cruel exercise of authority and power."[5] Many components of the job are unjust. The impact of trying to scramble to meet unjust expectations without adequate support crosses over into cruelty.

Teaching is an interesting idea to explore in the context of oppression, because we can see how our work is impacted by the "4 I's" of oppression: ideological, institutional, interpersonal, and internal. Most of this book focuses on helping educators re-author the oppressive attitudes and habits we have internalized. Because we didn't internalize them out of thin air, however, we'll also explore the ideologies, or systems of ideas, that deeply influence our experiences, but that are so common that sometimes we forget they are there. Institutions can be oppressive, usually in ways that show up in policies. Intrapersonal oppression, or unjust and cruel power dynamics between people, helps us understand why school cultures can so often be toxic. And it follows that, if someone is brought up in a culture where the unjust exercise of authority and power is a part of our dominant ideologies, our institutional policies, and our interpersonal interactions, it would be really, really hard not to internalize oppressive ideas.

Burnout

Of the three causes of professional discontent (burnout, demoralization, and exploitation), burnout is the easiest to identify, the quickest to remedy, and the speediest to heal after behavior change.

Burnout is a simple equation; energy out > energy in. It occurs when the energy we have available for a given task or idea is less than the energy the task or idea requires. We'll be grateful for burnout's reference to flame as a

---

[5] Merriam-Webster. (n.d.). Oppression. In Merriam-Webster.com dictionary. Retrieved March 27, 2022, from https://www.merriam-webster.com/dictionary/oppression

pneumonic device, as fuel is shorthand for stored energy. Over short periods, we can usually recover from energy discrepancies. For example, we may be exhausted after organizing community members as audience members for student presentations on a Friday, but if we can rest over the weekend and return enthusiastically, our overall energetic balance doesn't tip towards burnout. If, however, tiny daily imbalances don't have the chance to refresh over time, we'll experience the numb exhaustion characteristic of burnout.

Although burnout's causes are both individual and organizational, the blame is placed on individual teachers for allowing themselves to burn out. This blame inspired my immediate, defensive, shame-soaked denial that I might be burned out. Burnout is real and can have real impacts on your practice, your relationships, and yourself. While our culture overly blames the practitioner, especially when burnout is confused with demoralization and exploitation, there is some freedom in that single-person blaming: if individuals are the sources of their own burnout, so, too, can they be the sources of their own healing. To a point.

Burnout oversimplifies a complex range of symptoms and experiences with both environmental and biological causes. I am coming to understand both burnout and depression as diagnoses involving mental "metabolism;" in fact, the American Psychological Association has acknowledged burnout as a sort of work-induced depression.[6] As someone who also manages clinical depression (thank you diet, daily exercise, talk therapy, and medication), I want to be very clear. While there are concrete, specific behaviors that improve prognoses of both burnout and depression, individuals can't and shouldn't be blamed if and when the actions they take to remedy these conditions are insufficient to rebuild their energetic reserves. It's a nature vs. nurture question. Addressing burnout means addressing the energetic demands placed on a practitioner in context *and* examining practitioner behaviors and responses.

If a burned-out teacher has engaged all the self-care and mindfulness in the world and still wakes up with nightly panic attacks, I hope the whole world would support that teacher in choosing to leave teaching—and then

---

[6] Schonfeld, I. S., & Bianchi, R. (2016). Burnout and depression: Two entities or one? Journal of Clinical Psychology, 72(1), 22-37.

immediately get to work building a system in which any teacher would want to stay. But... I digress—and I dream. In the phone-parent vignette I offered earlier, while I maintain that burnout was not why I left the profession, I can still identify burnout in a few places. To see burnout, I look for evidence that I'm tired. Understandably, I was tired of heightened conflict with parents about enforcing school-wide policies sans administrator support (and which I was generally okay enforcing, as I didn't want students texting the day away, either). To address this, I could have better automated this process to make parental contact automatic (ex: a pre-drafted email that I could copy-and-paste). This would only have worked if I also committed to ensuring that each family had enough preemptive positive contact from me that, when a "your kid made a bummer choice" notification was in order, I had made enough "deposits" in the "Ms. Jess is on my side" account that it wouldn't break the bank.[7] I can find burnout in this example by identifying the places I could have worked smarter, not harder.

We started this list with burnout intentionally because it tends to be the easiest and most direct of the three maladies to address. Burnout is where you can start your own exploration of your relationship with your teaching practice, potentially with the least risk and most gain. A feeling of burnout in the classroom may not even need classroom-centric interventions. Burnout can sometimes be best-remedied by simply—and fully—protecting time for your to be yourself outside of teaching. Or by protecting time for you to learn who you are, if you're not yet sure.

Demoralization

> *"I want to become a teacher to force my students to lose their love of learning as painfully as possible."*
>
> *— No Educator, Ever —*

"Demoralization" was coined by Dr. Doris Santoro, who distinguished demoralization as a separate phenomenon from burnout.[8] Dr. Santoro, a curious philosopher who cares about public education and educators, interviewed hundreds of teachers who left the profession to construct her understanding of demoralization. Her work opened my eyes.

---

[7] Cline, F., & fay, J. (2020). Parenting with love and logic: teaching children responsibility. Navpress Publishing Group.
[8] Santoro, D. A. (2021). Demoralized: Why teachers leave the profession they love and how they can stay. Harvard Education Press.

Burnout may be an appropriate diagnosis in some cases where individual teachers' personal resources cannot meet the challenge of the difficulties presented by the work. However, the burnout explanation fails to account for situations where the conditions of teaching change so dramatically that moral rewards, previously available in ever-challenging work, are now inaccessible. In this instance, the phenomenon is better termed demoralization.

... In this model, teacher attrition does not necessarily reflect a lack of commitment, preparedness, competence, or hardiness on the part of the practitioner. Rather, teacher attrition is analyzed from the perspective of whether teachers find moral value in the kind of work they are asked to perform.[9]

I was not, on balance, burned out. I was demoralized. Even in the phone-parent vignette, which doesn't present as an obviously values-rich interaction, the demoralization is there.

We become demoralized when asked to act in service of values that conflict with the values that drew us to the profession.

Demoralization is an individual experience determined by an educator's individual moral commitments. Demoralization occurs, however, under the umbrella of institutional oppression; the institution's values are in conflict with each of our own. It's in the institution's best interest to maintain power, and if it does so by cruelly asking us to work in honor of values that aren't our own, the institution is both behaving oppressively and isn't terribly bothered.

Demoralization shows up in the phone-parent vignette in acute student safety concerns and in how my classroom structure undermined teacher-student relationships. Regarding safety, the National Science Foundation recommends a maximum class size of 24 students for lab work. In a class of 46, I risked students' physical safety for the experiential learning I value. Still, I'd be surprised if 5% of them remember any of freshman biology with any clarity, let alone fondness. So, at the bare minimum, I was leading a classroom in which students' safety and best instructional practices were in opposition. This moral dichotomy was a bummer, but it actually wasn't the

[9] Santoro, D. A. (2011). Good teaching in difficult times: Demoralization in the pursuit of good work. American Journal of Education, 118(1), 1-23.

one that pushed me over the demoralization edge.

For me, 46 students in each class was more demoralizing than a cause for burnout (though classes of 46 are exhausting). I cannot explain how, but I had the energy for it. What I did not have was the ability to contort what I knew about students and humans into a moral pretzel I could swallow. Given a 90-minute period (class every other day), less five minutes for the opener, ten minutes to get everyone situated, and three minutes to close, I had 72 instructional minutes available to connect with students as individual learners. This meant the maximum each student could get was 94 seconds of my individualized attention. Every other day. I was in the gig to connect with students and understanding what they need as individuals. Meaningful connection with individual students, given 94 seconds each, every other day, was an institutional impossibility.

Because I was not burned out, I had the energy to build group work, routinize classroom procedures (or try to... ahem... cell phone...), and find other workarounds to facilitate reasonable, accessible instruction to my average of 46 students per class. I got pretty good at it. However, developing skills to facilitate a classroom that could run without my intervention wasn't one of the values that drew me to the profession. My teaching goals were bigger than lessons in which no one cried or bled. I had higher expectations for myself, my students, and my practice. By my seventh year in the classroom, it didn't matter. My values didn't enter into the conversation. In order to survive my classroom, I wrote myself out of it—with severe consequences to my relationships with my loved ones, my students, myself, and my practice.

As teachers are neither valued via social status nor monetary compensation, I can look back now and see that the "good stuff" for me was my relationships with students. Those relationships were the whole dang point behind my major life decision to teach. As my classroom rosters grew, I traded relationships with students for instructional efficiency. I was trading away the very part that made teaching "worth it" to me. I believed then (and still believe) that students both need and crave adult mentorship, that students yearn for chances to explore how to be a person based on how they see personhood modeled. I do not think the most valuable thing students learn is how to follow directions to maximize behavioral compliance during a lab. I didn't believe it then, either, but you wouldn't know that by watching my efficient, compliance-dependent classroom.

Psychologist Robert Johnson argues that humans learn to value themselves by being valued.[10] I understood that my role was to "hold my students' gold" to show them how gorgeous, capable, essential and worthy they are until they're ready to believe it themselves and take their gold back. For holding their gold to work, however, they need to have understood and trusted me in that role. Rather, 80–90% of my students likely have no memory of me at all, let alone as someone who believed in them with such annoying persistence that they started believing in themselves.

It's not out of ego that I want students to remember me; it's an understanding of human psychology. I'm ok knowing that most of my thousands of students don't remember me at all. What I'm not okay with is that they will remember one less adult who saw, supported, and believed in them.

At least one remembers me solely as the witch who took her phone.

What Attracted You To Teaching?

Read through the following list.

Check each item that, at the starry-eyed, life-altering moment when you decided to become an educator, made your decision to teach begin to glow, alive, in your heart:

- ☐ Failing to meet students' learning needs due to a scripted curriculum or a mandated textbook
- ☐ Following school practices that increasingly focus on academic achievement even though students arrive at school with profound emotional needs
- ☐ Witnessing students feel worthless as their schools are graded/ranked/closed
- ☐ Being pressured by school leaders to pass students so schools can improve publicly available graduation rates
- ☐ Witnessing school leaders' rejection of teacher expertise and initiative in favor of adopting expensive products and services that yield dubious results
- ☐ Observing the increasing use of alternative and fast-track licensure programs that degrade and de-professionalize teaching[11]

No checkmarks? No problem. That's because zero teachers have ever entered the profession—though many have left—because of example

---

[10] Johnson, R. A. (2016). Inner gold: Understanding psychological projection. Chiron Publications.
[11] Santoro, D. A. (2018). Is it burnout? Or demoralization? Educational Leadership, 75(9), 3.

scenarios like those Santoro listed above.[12] Now, go through this list again, this time answering the question, "How many of these situations have you experienced?". If you've got a few checkmarks, you may want to tune in a bit more intentionally to the idea of demoralization. "Demoralization reaches its peak when teachers believe that they are violating basic expectations that educators should embody: do no harm to students, support student learning, and engage in professional behavior."[13]

If you're being asked to engage in policies, practices, or attitudes that hurt students, impede student learning, or violate professional ethics, demoralization may be the primary diagnosis for you. Caught it? Take heart. You'll write yourself a prescription as you explore your values—and ways they can inhabit more and more of your classroom—in Chapter 5.

Exploitation

Teachers, especially at the start of their career, are the most compassionate, moral folks I know (though we might be right up there with nurses, who engage in a similarly feminized profession).[14] Bummer for us, the opposite of compassionate morality is psychopathy.[15]

Psychopathy and compassionate morality go together like cake and ice cream—if we envision that the moral compassionate bakes, churns the ice cream, hand-decorates the cake with a celebratory message in a tidy script, then hands the plate over for the psychopathic system to devour. Messily. And without saying "thanks."

Important to note here; psychopathic individuals can participate in caring professions. Because helping professions are places where psychopaths find access to piles of morally compassionate people, actual psychopaths find their way into schools more often than we'd like to admit. Please be careful, and trust your gut in any relationship that makes you feel bad while you're earnestly trying your best.

Psychopathy is "a set of personality traits and behaviors frequently associated with lack of emotional sensitivity and empathy, impulsiveness, super-

---

[12] Wronowski, M. L. (2020). De-professionalized and demoralized: a framework for understanding teacher turnover in the accountability policy era. Leadership and Policy in Schools, 1-31.

[13] Santoro (2018). Is it burnout?, 2.

[14] Boyle, E. (2004). The feminization of teaching in America. Louis Kampf writing prize essay, Massachusetts Institute of Technology.

[15] Woodmass, K., & O'Connor, B. P. (2018). What is the opposite of psychopathy? A statistical and graphical exploration of the psychopathy continuum. Personality and Individual Differences, 131, 254-260.

ficial charm, and an inability to learn from experience."[16] For us moral compassionates, the mere existence of a person who is only looking out for "number one" is nearly impossible for us to understand. If we think of this metaphor in terms of the 4 I's of oppression, it's a bit easier to think of the system as behaving like a psychopathic individual; the ideologies and institutions we serve are self-serving. Power's guiding value is to maintain power. If those of us who are less concerned with power allow it, power for power's sake becomes a guiding systemic ideology.

From an evolutionary perspective, psychopaths co-evolved with those of us who are compassionately moral in a perfect balance.[17] To put it bluntly, there are givers and takers, and when we're not paying attention, it can seem like we need each other. The givers have tolerated the takers, tolerated the gaslighting and explained away the takers' bottomless selfishness and cruelty, like expert codependents.

Givers can learn to stop feeding the self-serving needs of a psychopath. But avoiding such codependency requires work on the part of the giver. The first step is to recognize when we're dealing with psychopathy. The U.S. public education system is, by definition, psychopathic. Why might we assign the education system, particularly public education, with such a harsh and stigmatized diagnosis as psychopathy? Because this book is, at its heart, about preventing further harm and initiating healing, we need truth-telling.

Let's break education's "psychopathic" diagnosis down by traits and behaviors. Psychopaths are charmers. The superficial charm of teaching is what caught you in the first place. A primary, though often unnamed appeal is teaching's familiarity; we know what teaching looks like because we watched two decades of it. Beyond familiarity, teaching also offers a chance for endless creativity and learning, the hopeful promise of autonomy over instructional decisions, and the chance to Make A Difference. Additionally, though some of us are more willing to admit it than others, the steady government gig with reliable benefits, limited direct supervision, and guaranteed holidays and unscheduled summers swept us off our non-entrepreneurial feet (please don't @ me with your "we don't get summers

---

[16] Hermann, H. R. (2017). Dominance and aggression in humans and other animals: The great game of life. Academic Press.

[17] Kinner, S. (2003). Psychopathy as an adaptation: Implications for society and social policy. In R. W. Bloom & N. Dess (Eds.), Evolutionary psychology and violence: A primer for policymakers and public policy advocates (pp. 57–81). Praeger Publishers/Greenwood Publishing Group.

off" defensiveness—we'll look at where that defensiveness comes from and why it might not serve you in Chapter 6).

Psychopaths regularly demonstrate both impulsiveness and an inability to learn from experience. American public education, too, has repeatedly demonstrated both impulsiveness and an inability to learn from experience. I entered the classroom in the heart of the No Child Left Behind (NCLB) era. Foolishly, I thought that the "accountability" measures and statistical manipulations that guided state, district, and school decision-making and separated my practice from my values were related to NCLB. I thought this because teacher prep programs don't teach us much about the history of education. They don't teach us much about what school is *for* or who decides what school is for. Rather, understandably and essentially, they teach us how to teach. As if teaching is a neutral endeavor. Welp, it's not. And control of the direction and velocity of public schooling has always been in the hands of those who benefit most from the system as-is.

Please read Dana Goldstein's *The Teacher Wars* if you haven't yet.[18] Ms. Goldstein's work explains that NCLB was the newest iteration of a cycle U.S. public schools have been looping since the late 1800s. Like other classic psychopaths, our system has not learned much from experience. We have been over-evaluating and under-exploring with our students as long as there has been a "we," as long as public education in the U.S. has been a thing.

Because the system doesn't learn from experience, we're vulnerable; we buy in when an academic builds their career on a previously understood idea that they've renamed. Once someone renames an idea, the impulsivity kicks in, usually in the form of sweeping initiatives and brand-new buzzwords. These initiatives come in reactionary waves, are unrolled with urgency, and are predictably left under-supported and floundering once the headlines and promotions are made. Which brings us to the public education system's lack of emotional sensitivity and empathy.

I have had lots of bosses, both human and institutional, who are able to make it sound like they have emotional sensitivity and empathy. Like psychopaths. (I'm not saying all of my bosses were psychopaths—but I'm not saying none were, either.) Invariably, they have explicitly and empathetically said things like "teachers work too hard—y'all should take some time off."

---

[18] Goldstein, D. (2015). The teacher wars: A history of America's most embattled profession. Anchor.

Also invariably, those same administrators judge, critique, or actually prevent their same educators from doing things like actually taking time off.

Once, I was hired specifically for my commitment and ability to teach lab- and activity-centric science. I was also not assigned a classroom in which to facilitate said lab- and activity-centric science. I sprinted between six different borrowed classrooms spread across three different floors, using classrooms that were temporarily empty during other teachers' prep periods, pushing a 300 lb. cart of lab notebooks, glassware, etc. After two months of this madness, I went to the principal with a potential solution: I could work with colleagues to share two rooms where I could leave student materials. At the close of my argument, my principal looked up from cleaning his glasses (actually) and said, "There, now. Don't you feel better getting that off of your chest?" I did not feel better. I still did not have a classroom. But he sounded so empathetic...

The only thing worse than being denied emotional sensitivity and empathy when working an emotionally draining and empathetically complex job is being gaslit about that denial. Educators experience this systemically. It happened when, during my colleagues' bi-weekly appointment to sell his plasma for supplementary income, the clinician managing his IV thanked him for his service. It happened when another colleague was berated by a parent for leaving a dance performance early—a school night dance performance of one of her 180 8th graders at a non-school event during a week in which she also attended a student's soccer game and another's quinceañera. It happened when I was delivering make-up assignments to the home of one of my students who had broken her arm in a car accident two days prior. Her mom thanked me for coming and asked why I took so long.

Psychopaths freely express gratitude as a manipulative maneuver, quickly crossing into anger when their expressions don't get them more of what they want. The culture, the structures, and the people adjacent to public education express support—when it costs them nothing and gets them more of what they need. When educators also need things, that support is often withdrawn. We see this in the phone incident; my ability to hyper-manage an overcrowded classroom was exploited by my administrators and the larger system, who kept my class sizes unreasonably large while denying me the structural backup to uphold school-wide policies meant to keep the place running. I know we're dealing with exploitation here because I was put in the position of enforcing my administration's policy, fielding a parent's displeasure about the policy, and then being scolded for the parent's displeasure. If I had been in a reciprocal, non-exploitative relationship with the system, my administrator would have defended the policy, left me out of it, and fielded the parent's displeasure themselves.

The bottom line is this: school systems tend to be takers, and teachers tend to be givers. School systems lean towards the psychopathic, and teachers lean towards moral compassion. In a head-to-head competition between psychopaths and not psychopaths, psychopaths will always win.

Does this mean you have to stop teaching? No. You do not need to stop teaching. You need to stop pretending you're teaching in what could or should be a supportive community, make a few changes, and keep right on teaching. Unlike person-to-person relationships, you're in a person-to-system relationship with a psychopathic system. The clinical advice for dealing successfully with psychopaths is clear; don't.[19] Because we know the system is psychopathic and relationships with psychopaths aren't survivable, you need to end your relationship with the system. This is different than ending your relationship with your teaching practice.

Separating your own teaching practice from the system in which you teach can be tough for people who are morally compassionate. When teachers do it badly or without support, they quit in reactionary ways instead of through intentionally responsive planning. They quit everything mid-year and find minimum wage work, sacrificing significant retirement-related benefits. They start emotionally charged and damaging conversations with colleagues that lead to ongoing stress-inducing interactions during meetings and in the copy room. More frequent than explosive reactivity, and differently damaging, well-meaning practitioners most often just completely check out. They're technically in the room, but investing little in their instruction, students, collegial relationships, or school.

While I understand what motivates approaches like these, I don't recommend them. They're great ways to stack up regrets to meet you on your deathbed. Thankfully, these types of options aren't your only options.

---

[19] Clarke, J. (2009). Working With Monsters: How to Identify and Protect Yourself from the Workplace Psychopath: Easyread Edition. ReadHowYouWant.com.

Separating yourself from the system while still working within it can look like measured, self-assured liberation. In order to liberate yourself, you've got to be extremely honest with yourself about your situation.

Before burnout, teachers tend to be collaborative. We want to be and believe we are part of a larger team, a giant, supportive structure that has our backs as we do the backbreaking, boots-on-the-ground, hard work. Those of us who believe this are wrong. Those of us who have rejected it only to be consumed by bitter rage and isolation, however, are no better off than we who are naïvely mistaken.

The trick is to both acknowledge that the system isn't for you and stop wanting or expecting it to be any different.

By understanding that you are not in relationship with the system, you can navigate it like you do other unwieldy, potentially harmful structures. Think, for example, about the IRS. No one expects warm, cuddly feelings from the IRS. We expect to be misunderstood, to have to represent ourselves impeccably. We hope to honor our obligation and interact minimally. The IRS is there to extract from us. We know this, so we frame our relationship accordingly. It's high time we acknowledge that the U.S. public education system is built to do the same—it's built to extract from educators maximally. It's then up to us, teacher by teacher, to draw a line. Just as we contribute to the IRS, we educators wish to contribute to the public education system at a reasonable, survivable level to support the common good. Like damn fools, though, we've been signing over our metaphorical bank balances. But we don't have to do that anymore.

We don't have to be angry and hurt that the system doesn't give a hoot about us. We can simply acknowledge that it doesn't. We don't have to worry about how we caused the system to behave psychopathically—we didn't; it just does (for now). Now that we have been honest about the nature of the relationship, we get to make some choices:

If you walk into the yard once and are bitten, the dog has bitten you.
If you walk into the yard a second time and are bitten, you have bitten you.
This very awareness can change everything[20]

---

[20] Katie, B., & Mitchell, S. (2008). A thousand names for joy: Living in harmony with the way things are. Harmony.

Activity: Diagnosis—The First Step Towards Healing

The checklist below offers a list of possible experiences and reactions to burnout, demoralization, and exploitation, respectively. Give it a read and check off any statements that describe you and your experience. This list hasn't been rigorously, empirically tested and validated. It is not evidence-based practice. Rather, it's sourced from practitioner experience, from practice-based evidence. It's a place for you to start asking yourself about these potential negative impacts on your practice and your well-being. It's a tool to get you in the habit of noticing because we've got to notice something before we can address it.

Burnout

Place a checkmark by any of the statements that apply to you, particularly with respect to your teaching practice during the school year:

- ☐ I rarely feel rested.
- ☐ I forget or mishandle my own important personal affairs (paying bills, registering vehicles, etc).
- ☐ I have little energy for my personal life after work.
- ☐ I don't care if it makes me a bad teacher, I leave at the end of my paid contract day whether I'm ready for the next school day or not.
- ☐ I do not exercise (I mean nothing—not even a walk around the block).
- ☐ I have difficulty falling asleep, and/or I wake up in the middle of the night with anxiety about all of the tasks I have yet to complete.
- ☐ I say 'no' whenever anyone asks me to do anything extra without listening to or considering what it is.
- ☐ I speak to people that I love with sharpness or impatience that I'm not proud of.
- ☐ I frequently feel overwhelmed.
- ☐ I am so stressed about getting stuff done that I'm less efficient in actually getting stuff done.

Demoralization

Place a checkmark by any of the statements which apply to you, particularly with respect to your teaching practice during the school year:

- ☐ I am obligated to use scripted curricula, but I'd rather not.
- ☐ I am obligated to use a curriculum I dislike.
- ☐ I have little control over how my classroom time is spent.
- ☐ I am unable to sufficiently respond to my students who need help, both inside and outside of the classroom.
- ☐ I am concerned about the harm that other colleagues in my school are causing to my students.
- ☐ I feel I am causing my students harm with the amount of testing I am required to facilitate.
- ☐ I carry negative feelings about students whose performance may negatively impact my data.
- ☐ I am evaluated on the parts of my practice that I don't believe are the most impactful for student outcomes.
- ☐ I am frequently critiqued, but I am not often offered suggestions for how to improve, nor am I acknowledged for what I do well.
- ☐ It's hard for me to focus on my teaching because of all of the forms, meetings, activities, and additional responsibilities expected of me by my school, district, and state.

Exploitation

Place a checkmark by any of the statements which apply to you, particularly with respect to your teaching practice during the school year:

- ☐ I spend most of Sunday dreading Monday.
- ☐ I feel anxious about my professional relationships with colleagues and administrators.
- ☐ When parents complain, administrators rarely defend or support me.
- ☐ I spend personal money and time on school-related materials.
- ☐ I no longer attempt to contribute ideas during professional meetings because it's unsafe to do so, and my ideas aren't considered.
- ☐ I am constantly aware of how I could be doing things better, and that awareness causes me stress.
- ☐ I am not supported by my administration in school policy enforcement.
- ☐ There are multiple examples of unequal resource distribution among teachers in my school.
- ☐ My administrators have "favorite" educators who clearly receive a different level of support than other educators.
- ☐ I am expected (explicitly or implicitly) to volunteer for committees, after-school support, or other school-related activities.

Prescription

Tally your scores from the checklists above to determine the likely impact that burnout, demoralization, and/or exploitation is having on your practice:

Burnout =   /10
Demoralization =   /10
Exploitation =   /10

Use your relative scores to determine which phenomena may be more or less impactful to your practice. Use this information to tailor your self-care as you continue through the book.

What To Do About It: An Overview

While the remaining chapters will go into more detail regarding the cause, effect, and especially how to remedy the your pained relationship with your practice, the following table serves as a guide for how to think about and address these three sources of pain:

	Burnout	Demoralization	Exploitation
Causes	Using more energy than you have	Acting in a manner that is different from (or opposed to) the values that drew you into the profession	Being taken advantage of by people and systems serving their own aims without regard for you or yours
Internal Interventions	Be honest about your energy budget Craft internal boundaries regarding tasks and time	Name the values that drew you to the profession and the values you currently wish to enact	Be honest about the nature of your professional relationships Craft internal boundaries regarding relationships (both with people and with structures)
External Interventions	Increase your efficiency, particularly in non-essential tasks Prioritize strategic physical self-care	Find ways to enact your values in your daily teaching practice—and do so Prioritize intentional spiritual and emotional self-care	Modify your interpersonal and systemic interactions Prioritize intentional social and emotional self-care

For the rest of the book, we'll refer to the career-impacting (or ending) triumvirate of burnout, demoralization, and exploitation as BD&E.

Too Long; Didn't Read
Chapter 2:
Burnout vs. Demoralization vs. Exploitation

Ideas

- **Burnout is an energy issue.** Burnout is caused by an energy imbalance created when we spend energy faster than we can adequately refuel.
- **Demoralization is an alignment issue.** Demoralization is caused by acting out of alignment with the values that drew us to the profession in the first place (we are asked to act in opposition to our values).
- **Exploitation is a contracting issue.**
  Exploitation is caused by teachers' helper natures being taken advantage of by a system that will continue to take.

Strategies

- **Burnout is cured by:**
- ◆ Taking an earnest, honest inventory of all of the tasks and patterns of thinking that consume your energy and all of the activities and practices that refuel you.
- ◆ Eliminating tasks and obligations when possible, and modifying required tasks and obligations to be as low-demand as possible.
  Scheduling and enacting intentional refueling activities.
- ◆ Honoring your refueling plans as you do your other obligations.
- **Demoralization is cured by:**
- ◆ Naming the values that currently inspire your practice.
- ◆ Naming the values motivating the meaningless/harmful tasks.
- ◆ Intentionally disengaging with harmful values
- ◆ Focusing on enacting the values that motivate your practice in clear, observable ways in your classroom daily.
- **Exploitation is cured by:**
- ◆ Shifting your view of schools, districts, and state structures from relational sources of support to necessary regulatory agencies.
- ◆ Building and enacting internal and external boundaries to honor your contract with excellence, but no more.

Chapter 3

Teachers: Amazing Grown-Ups, Crappy Adults

In which we examine how educators are—and aren't—"professionalized," and how that process is currently facilitated in a manner that contributes to BD&E.

> *"Psychological and spiritual adulthood does not come automatically with age. It requires ongoing and ardent work on ourselves."*
> — David Richo —[21]

I was fortunate to find at least one veteran educator willing to take me under their wing in every school where I taught. These educators have been kind, dedicated, and earnest. Some were paid a whopping $500 per year (sarcasm) to play an official mentorship role in my early-career induction. Some volunteered; I imagine supporting me was one way they were working to remoralize their own imperiled practices. They gave me the following advice (verbatim):

- "Don't trust administrators. They're just out to build their resumes, use you, and be on their way."
- "Pay as much attention to the things you already do well as the things you want to improve."
- "Don't smile [at your students] until after Winter Break."
- "The kids who are the hardest to love are the ones who need it the most."
- "Stop working so hard. You're making us all look bad."
- "The three best things about teaching are June, July, and August."
- "Trust your students as people who really want to learn."
- "Whenever anyone asks you to do something extra, just say 'no'."

---

[21] Richo, D. (1991). How to be an adult: A handbook on psychological and spiritual integration. Paulist Press.

Can you find a pattern? I couldn't.

Though I couldn't identify a unifying theme behind the statements above, I think I understand the motivation behind each. The "don't work so hard" and "June, July, August" bits scream burnout. Ideas about not smiling and loving kids were conflicting attempts to address demoralization. Caution about overcommitting and believing admins' promises revealed how my colleagues had taught themselves to guard against exploitation.

The unifying theme may simply be that, through these instructions, my colleagues were doing their best as mentors, as my teacher preparation program did its best. I was as prepared as I could have been for my early years in the classroom—but totally unprepared for the realities that impacted my life during my lunch breaks, in the hallways, in the faculty meetings and parking lot conversations, and in my personal life.

Grad school is intended to teach you the theoretical frameworks behind the decisions one might make in the classroom. Unfortunately, there's not much time dedicated to helping early-career teachers anticipate the menu of actual choices when it comes to grading, planning, implementing, and evaluating instruction. If there isn't time for that, there certainly isn't time to teach us all how to become adults.

Teacher Professionalization is Accidental—and Harmful

Joining a faculty is reminiscent of movie renditions of what it looks like to begin a prison sentence. There's instantaneous sizing up. Various cliques bid to either recruit or reject the rookie. There are hazing rituals (for teachers, this looks like being given the crappiest room, the least survivable schedule, etc.). Battle lines have been drawn before the new recruit even arrives. There are expectations of—and consequences for—the rookie educator, whether they grab a weapon, attempt to make peace, or stay out of the fray entirely.

Faculty-to-faculty vitriol, sabotage, and general negativity is a painful, real, and predictable side effect of adults being managed by a psychopathic, resource-constrained system. It's lateral violence; the way oppression perpetuates interpersonally. And it's perpetuated because veteran educators who have been harmed by the system, who are surviving their own burnout, demoralization, and exploitation (BD&E), are tasked with mentoring the new generation—without any additional training or meaningful support.

Mentoring is an essential, complex skill that requires instruction, modeling, observation, and critique in continuous-improvement cycles. Mentor teachers are not offered this support. Instead, they're asked to usher in the next generation of educators by squeezing the task into their lunch breaks. In the absence of the support the role deserves, mentor teachers do their best by teaching what they know. They do this, however, without embedded professional support to examine their own biases, weaknesses, and relationships to power. They do this without clear expectations nor goals from the districts that process their reports. And they do it without an obligation to help their mentees improve.

Beyond the formal-but-unsupported mentorship structures, many powerful professionalizing interactions occur in informal settings. What we're told in passing in hallways, while waiting at the copy machine, or in line for the microwave in the teachers' lounge can have significant impacts on the way we view our practice, our role within a school or team, even our relationships with our students, administrators, and colleagues. Like the rest of human interaction, dominant power structures are the default if we don't weigh in intentionally to balance the scales. Leaving teacher professionalization up to haphazard interactions between harried, overburdened, under-supported colleagues sets up the system to perfectly replicate itself, building generation after generation of burned-out, demoralized, exploited "support."

Your Colleagues Are Not Your Friends

Teaching is a lonely gig. Rather than being reliable sources of support, our collegial interactions often contribute significantly to our work-related stress. I used to oversimplify this by excusing collegial misbehavior as my colleagues' threat responses to working in resource-constrained environments. Resource constraint is a real and constant experience for the public educator. It will almost always bring out the most competitive, selfish, and petty parts of people. We can forgive them and ourselves for being forced to gladiate for a classroom with windows, functional classroom furniture, or a survivable schedule. But don't confuse forgiveness for being on the same team, that they have your back. Nothing—not money, incentives, nor evaluation—nothing incentivizes your colleagues to be good to you.

Burnout, demoralization, and exploitation (BD&E) increase our collea-gues' tendencies to isolate, disengage, micromanage, manipulate, gossip, power grab, and administratively gaslight. Unfortunately, our de facto professionalization means that we're all a few frustrating faculty meetings away from behaving like 5-year-old versions of ourselves. The reasons for this are embedded in the very role the profession asks us to inhabit while we're "in front of" the class.

Many of Us Are Grown-Ups, Few of Us Are Adults

Growing up is inevitable. Becoming an Adult is a choice. Many people confuse the two, as this isn't a space our public, secular culture acknowl-edges much, so we'll explore the difference. From here on out, we'll use "grown-up" to describe someone who is simply physically grown and temporally mature, and we'll use "adult" to describe someone who has done the additional internal work of figuring out who they are, who they want to be, and how they'll behave to stay in alignment with those truths.

Educators are structurally permitted, even encouraged, to skip becoming adults because they step immediately from the role of student to the role of teacher. By definition, the teacher is an adult, right? Unfortunately, no. Many of us are just grown-ups. Being a teacher is a role, and only a role.

Many educators confuse our roles for our identities without discovering who we are separate from our roles.

This sets us up to have really high expectations of ourselves—or at least expectations that overly align with one part of our lives, often at high cost to the rest of our lives. It is also a setup, as our over-identification as educators usually corresponds with our wildly inaccurate expectations about how the profession will care for us—and we fall hard when our expectations are not met. When we're let down, either by ourselves or the system, we're vulnerable to BD&E. We're just grownups, assuming that everyone around us is an adult, not knowing how they got there or why we aren't with them.

To get at these ideas, we will use a few tools from Jungian psychology, specifically ideas about Inner parts and individuation. You've heard of the "Inner Child," yes? Unfortunately, the Inner Child idea can feel cliché due to its popularity in pop psychology. We'll polish it up because the Inner

Child is an extremely helpful idea for educators—as is the Inner Parent. Most important is what Jung called the Self, which we'll call the Inner Adult. We come pre-loaded from childhood with an Inner Child and an Inner Parent. We need to grow our own Inner Adult—but precious few of us do.

Your Inner Child is the part of you that wants things. Your Inner Child is the part of you that knows what feels good, what is fun, that is connected to the moment. A healthy Inner Child allows us freedom and safety to feel emotions deeply and fully. Our Inner Child helps us tune in to living a life true to ourselves.

Educators who are more connected with their Inner Child, but who have not yet cultivated their Inner Adult, tend to do things like skip out on meetings (and fib about the reason why). Someone with a strong Inner Child tends to skew on the side that looks out at the world and blames the world for their problems. Someone with a vulnerable Inner Child is likely to internalize oppressive work conditions and turn them into messages about what a bad job they're doing all of the time, what a terrible teacher they are, and how they can't ever do anything right. That's what unjust and cruel power systems sound like when they become integrated with your internal parts.

Our Inner Parent's voice is a compilation of our own caretakers' voices as well as cultural and societal messages about who we should be. Educators with a strong Inner Parent, but who lack an Inner Adult, are less connected to what they actually want and are more connected to what they "should" want, what they "should" do, and who they "should" be. Our Inner Parent is the part of us that is the most susceptible to internalized oppression with respect to our performance as educators. Educators with strong Inner Parent voices are constantly berating themselves about what they should be doing instead of what they are doing and how everything should have been better than it is. They experience a punishing sense of responsibility; when things go wrong for these educators, in ways that life never goes perfectly, they blame themselves.

Cultivating an Inner Adult is how we bridge the gap from grown-up to adult. All of us have access to an Inner Parent and an Inner Child, and it's essential to recognize the voice of each—but it's neither effective nor fun to let either take over. We cultivate an Inner Adult by helping our Inner Child and Inner Parent talk to each other; the Inner Adult serves as a mediator. It can sound like this: "Inner Child, I get that you've had a hard day and just want to watch TV. Inner Parent, we did have a rough day, and it's not helpful when you call us lazy. Let's listen to a guilty-pleasure podcast while we go for a walk to burn off some stress." This Inner conversation, while seemingly simple and even obvious, can feel nearly impossible to educators, particularly if we don't yet know how to identify these different voices, let alone how to interact with them.

Our species' typical developmental arc follows a predictable pattern; we are physically children first, then we are independent grown-ups, then we become parents (on average across our species). In this generic storyline, we have a chance to embody an outer adult as we learn to cultivate an Inner Adult. Teachers' developmental arcs, however, are different. Professionally, we are students (assuming the role of Inner Children), then we become teachers (assuming the role of Inner Parents). We skip a step. We aren't explicitly supported to build our Inner Adult before being put in a position of authority and responsibility.

We build identities as a Teachers, which are more aligned with authoritarian Inner Parents than assertive Inner Adults.

Why do our Inner Parents skew authoritarian? As teachers, in addition to all of the normal familial and societal expectations informing our personal Inner Parent voices, we are also conduits for all of the cultural "shoulds." To be an educator in a nation that has yet to decide what school is actually for is to field wildly variable expected outcomes. We feel like we need to create an equitable learning space in which students learn to work in teams while cultivating their individuality. We get messages to individuate instruction and are simultaneously asked to get every student across the same standardized exam finish line. It's on us to build citizens worthy of participatory democracy while we're expected to run our classrooms like dictatorships. We're to involve families without overburdening them, behave in a manner that's above reproach but isn't clearly defined, and negotiate extreme dynamism in how we're supported while providing unwavering support to our students. We are to build critical thinkers who will also be obedient employees. These consistent-but-conflicting messages directly inform our Inner life and is often the script our own Inner Parent recites to us—disapprovingly. Educators governed by Inner Parents feel accountable to all of those expectations.

When I ask an educator to justify a particular classroom management strategy or instructional choice, their response is frequently something like, "It's my job to build these people into functional human beings who can become contributing members of society," or, "The health of our democracy depends on this assignment." Whoa. That's a lot of pressure. We have been put in the position of proxy parent by a culture that sometimes expects us to fulfill that role, sometimes resents us for that role, and has little interest in helping us to cultivate a healthy, individuated sense of self to enact that role with grace, humor, and calm self-regulation.

Without an Inner Adult, We Are Harmed—And Cause Harm

Teacher-as-identity has consequences both for our personal lives and for the profession itself. By identifying as educators before we have figured out who we are as adults, we risk under-identifying with our peers, friends, family, and communities who aren't educators and at risk of over-identifying with our roles. We risk mistaking our roles for our identities altogether.

Over-identifying with our teacher roles motivates our burnout, demoralization and exploitation (BD&E). Identity-related vulnerability to BD&E can be driven by both Inner Child and Inner Parent. Our Inner Child can drive us to harm to our students by over-rejecting the structures imposed on us by the system to the point that we actually stop doing a good job as educators. We see this in our colleagues who cope with their BD&E by playing an awful lot of videos, scrolling through social media while their students "do worksheets," and denying students feedback because they've deemed grading "too much work." Our Inner Parent's criticism can push us to self-harming perfectionism. In a profession of endless to-do lists, an Inner Parent who will only shut up when everything is crossed off is unsurvivable.

While the Inner Parent is easiest to blame, both our Inner Child and Inner Parent can actually motivate workaholism. Our Inner Child can drive us to overwork because our Inner Child craves connection. We do earnestly enjoy our students, and often our students' affections and attentions can feel easier to access and be more immediately rewarding than our own complex adult relationships. Our Inner Parent can drive our workaholism when we're compelled to overwork due to internal messages of our own worthlessness, fraudulence, or our core (perceived) undeserving nature. If we aren't cultivating a strong Inner Adult to help manage how we respond to these compulsions to overwork, we can look up ten years later, with aching joints, bruised family relationships, and without having had an honest conversation with a trusted friend in who-knows-how-long.

We see evidence that teachers haven't cultivated their Inner Adults when we watch them in professional learning settings. Those of us who haven't yet done this internal work will immediately turn into the very student that pushes our own buttons. You've seen it, I'm sure. Colleagues who rage about students' phones all day, then sit on their own phones through faculty meetings. Educators who police their own students' social interactions then speak sharply to their colleagues' faces and gossip behind their backs. If there isn't an Inner Adult to run the show, it's our Inner Parents who help us to act like teachers all day. When we're not leading a classroom, it's like our Inner Children have been repressed in the service of our Inner Parents; when the pressure of that role is removed, our Inner Parent is off the clock; we regress to that immature version of ourselves as our Inner Child takes over.

Beyond making us more functional and comfortable, cultivating an Inner Adult benefits our students. Without an Inner Adult, our Inner Parent can react with anger, spite, and power-obsessed words and actions. Acting from our Inner Parents can leave students momentarily paralyzed in fear and traumatized for life. Without cultivating an Inner Adult, our Inner Child wants our students to be our friends. While we certainly want to be friendly, being friends with our students is not our role. It's unfair to burden our students with the responsibility of managing our feelings. It's unfair to task students with figuring out how to safely field our inappropriate over-disclosures. Educators with an unchecked Inner Child feed off of the admiration, idolization, and fawning that students can offer teachers; educators ruled by an Inner Child can explain all manner of damaging educator-student relationships, including those involving statutory rape.

Supporting students to become who they're becoming is a sacred obligation. No matter what you believe school is for. Because you have chosen to accept this beautifully challenging work, you have a responsibility to both your students and yourself to cultivate your Inner Adult.

Your Inner Adult is the grounded, reliable part of yourself that will allow you to teach in connection with your values through grace, humor, and well-supported high expectations for your students. Your Inner Adult is your vehicle to become the teacher you want to be—and to stay that way.

Both Professionalization and Individuation Are Inside Jobs

There's a trick to keep in mind when talking to people who feel stuck. It works as well with adolescent students overwhelmed by setting up a word problem as it does adults facing a major life decision. If they respond to a question with, "I don't know," counter with, "Fair. But what would you do if you did know?"

Just like we can cultivate an Inner Adult to re-parent a neglected or abused Inner Child to heal from early-life trauma, we can also conjure mentorship for ourselves.[22] We can envision what our ideal mentor would provide us and use that as the model for what our Inner Adult provides us. Hard work? Yes! Extremely empowering? You betcha.

Complaining about a "broken," harmful, inefficient, damaging, and maddening system doesn't change it. While doing so may connect us with our Inner Child's wants and our Inner Parent's view of how the world should be, neither of those Inner voices shift our relationship to the problem. To reject Burnout, Demoralization, and Exploitation—and step fully into our power as Inner-Adult-cultivating-educators—we've got to acknowledge that no one is coming to save us.

No one will do this work for us. We have do this work for ourselves.

So, let's get started! Shall we?

---

22 LePera, N. (2021). How to do the work: recognize your patterns, heal from your past, and create your self. HarperCollins.

Too Long; Didn't Read
Chapter 3: Teachers: Amazing Grown-Ups, Crappy Adults

Ideas

- Teacher professionalization is poorly supported and haphazard.
- Every teacher carries an Inner Child (things we want/need) and an
- Inner Parent (things our world told us we should do or be).
- Healthy development requires cultivating an Inner Adult who can mediate between the Inner Child and Inner Parent.
- Haphazard professionalization leaves many educators with strong Inner Children (selfish and extractive) and Inner Parents (scolding and resentful), but without Inner Adults who can support us to make sound, loving decisions both in the moment and over time.

Strategies

- Name the parts of you that are motivated by an Inner Child. Explore your tendency to either deny or indulge that Inner Child, and how those tendencies may impact the way you relate to both yourself and your students.
- Name the parts of you that are motivated by an Inner Parent. Evaluate the likelihood that your Inner Parent's influence on your views of how the world "should" be may be contributing to your suffering.
- Cultivate an Inner Adult to help your Inner Child and Inner Parent agree on how to self-regulate and maneuver in an imperfect world in a way that aligns with who you'd like to be.

Chapter 4

Boundaries Are Necessary and Nurturing

In which we define boundaries, figure out why they make some of us so uncomfortable, and learn why boundaries are one of the most important pieces of our teaching practice, no matter the values that motivate that practice.

*"Boundaries are the distance at which
I can love you and me simultaneously."*
— Prentis Hemphill —

Setting Boundaries is Scary

Educators are, by nature, helpers. While different teachers enact their help-ing nature in different ways, assuming an educator's essential identification with being a helper is a reasonably safe bet. Being a helper isdifferent than being helpful. While some people may have helping impulses, like a software developer who wants to help people use phones to bank more efficiently, educators tend to want to help in exchange for a different currency than software developers. Software developers, for example, tend to want actual currency. Educators tend to demand less of that. Instead, they not only accept, but they crave, and will beg, borrow, or steal for their preferred currency—appreciation.

We like being liked. We want to be wanted. Some of us, still early in the cultivation of our Inner Adult, even need to be needed. What's wrong with that? Nothing, in moderation. And when unchecked, everything.

If our identity, our sense of value as people, is wrapped up in how much others seem to appreciate us, then other people determine our value. If other people get to decide our value, then they get to set the bar. Because you volunteer to help students at lunch, you might be willing to do so after school as well, right? Because you did such a great job on that task force, you seem like a natural "pick" for that additional committee. That's a slippery slope, right there; I've set myself up so that the only measure of my self-worth is in how much I (try to) please other people. If my sense of self-worth is connected to the approval of people I cannot control, particularly those who benefit from my overworking, it's hard to say "no." When we bind our self-worth to other people's perceptions of us, we allow the threat of disapproval to motivate choices that do not serve us, nor, ultimately, our students, in the long run.

The system is expert at exploiting educators' natural inclinations to be helpers; it relies on our paired desires to be both effective and approved of. We want to be effective, and our efficacy is measured by inappropriate instruments. When those instruments communicate that we are ineffective, we accept that judgement as if it is right or meaningful. We see this in educators who are distressed by end-of-level exams. In my entire career in public education, during which I knew and directly worked with hundreds of teachers, I never knew one educator who lost their job due to student scores on end-of-level exams alone. Unfortunately, I did know some who were discussed in hushed tones by hand-wringing administrators or shamed publicly in faculty meetings. While I wouldn't wish either of those experiences on my colleagues, I saw those interactions inspire heights of anxiety about the security of our positions that far exceeded the actual threat.

One can have a humiliating meeting or have one's boss talk behind their back and still be able to pay for groceries and maintain health insurance coverage. Being dismissed, misunderstood, or even disliked in the workplace isn't the same as being fired. It's not fair, it's not right, but it's our decision how much power we'd like to give these inevitable injustices over our own experience. Rather than tolerating an uncomfortable situation while focusing on the work that feeds us, however, we often allow ourselves to whip into a frenzy that our students' shoddy exam scores will get us fired. These frenzies push us to work even harder to prevent the dire consequences that we (the overwhelming amount of the time) imagine. Why do we give these experiences such power? It's simple; we don't generally learn how to do anything different. Without intervention, our default wiring wins.

Our Brains Impact Our Boundaries

Why do we allow ourselves to get so worked up over empty threats? Why does it hurt so badly to feel rejected? It all has to do with the way the human brain was built.

Our responses to our experiences of threat in our workplaces are artifacts of our evolution as a social species. Our brains have been in their current configuration for approximately 200,000 years, but our lives look slightly different today than they did all those millennia ago. Before we explore the impacts of our evolutionary history on our current brains and behaviors, however, let's address two common misunderstandings about evolution: Evolution, as a process, does not work towards some ideal goal, and "survival of the fittest" is on a per-trait basis. Rather, evolution is a bit haphazard and accidental. It's more like "survival of the second-to-most-crappy or that which worked well enough at the time."

To understand how evolutionary history impacts our brains, and therefore us, let's think of our brains like my house. During the majority of its 100 year history, the neighborhood in which the house sits has been decidedly working class. The house is not fancy. Nothing about it is "top of the line." Changes were made out of necessity, meant to get as far as possible as cheaply as possible. The walls are covered in lumpy plaster that was easier and cheaper to glob on than taking the time to do a nice job finishing the drywall. Bathroom tile adorns the fireplace. The back porch was framed in at some point when someone needed more space; the sloping molding leans into the difference between how the clay under the porch settled compared to the foundation. No one scraped off the previous wallpaper before applying more—peeling off the layers was archeological. My personal favorite? Someone installed tile over carpet.

Evolution's remodeling approach is similar to the many people who have called this place home before we did. Evolution doesn't actually go for best, it goes for efficient and "good enough." No need to get rid of the previous layer and good enough is good enough. Our brains' remodels look a lot like the layering approach of the tile over carpet. It was easier to leave the part of our brains that we have in common with reptiles, which runs our basic physiology, than it was to "figure out" how to get rid of it. The analogy falls apart here, however, as the older parts of our brain do play the same essential roles as when they were the dominant manner of functioning. As we became increasingly social as a species, we still needed our hearts to beat and lungs to expand and deflate, and so that part of the brain stuck around as we added on. The trouble is, when we added on, we effectively froze those older parts of our brain in a state that doesn't match the world as we experience it today.

Our brains, thank goodness, are parts of our bodies. Our bodies are the bits that responded when, over millennia, our reptilian brains would initiate a shot of stress hormones, which allowed us to turbocharge our body's response. Our fight-flight-or-freeze response has been effective. Those who have strong stress responses were able to make more babies because they survived whatever threat it was by either beating the threat, escaping the threat, or tolerating the threat without dying.

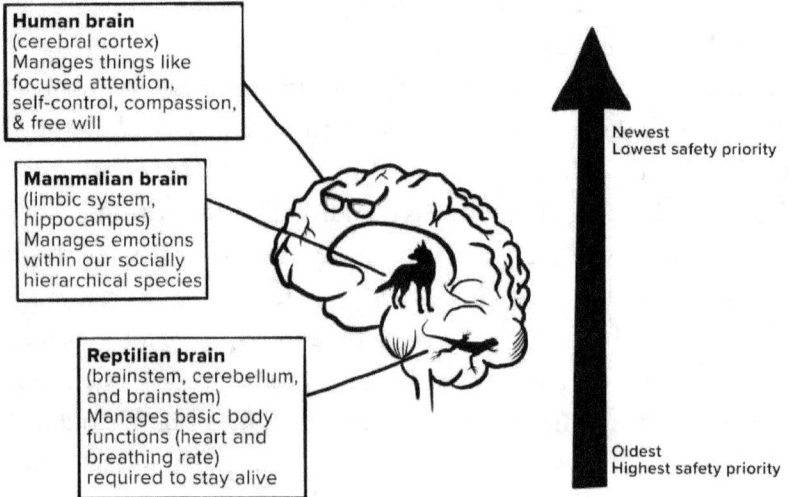

The problem is that we still have a part of our brain that initiates this fight-flight-or-freeze response no matter the size, type, or realness of any given threat. Our alarm clock sounds (cue stress hormones). Someone cuts us off during our commute (cue stress hormones). We think about something stressful (cue stress hormones). "We are equipped with 200,000-year-old hardware trying to download 21st-century software."[23] This mismatch between how we're wired and how we're expected to work leaves us in a state of chronic stress.

---

[23] Clear, J. (2018). Atomic habits: An easy & proven way to build good habits & break bad ones. Avery.

Social Threats Feel Like Survival Threats

The plot thickens. As a social species, our evolutionary survival depended on how much our fellow upright-walking brain-remodelers liked hanging out with us. For humans, and for around 1.5 million years of hominid existence before us, we experienced a social threat with the same intensity as any other existential threat. Doing something wrong enough to piss off the hominid in charge, wrong enough to get kicked out, was a death sentence. If you didn't perish once you were kicked out of the tribe (because of exposure, being killed by a warring group, or being consumed by a more fearsome predator), you certainly weren't going to pass on your rebel, stick-it-to-the-man genes as you wandered the wilderness alone. Hence the social utility of guilt and shame. Guilt and shame are social tools used to keep hierarchical species like ours in social relationship. Our genes don't care how it makes us feel as long as they keep getting passed on.

And all of this is why setting boundaries is scary.

Every time we set a boundary, we risk disrupting another human's expectations of us. Historically, this disruption could have gotten us killed. And we kept, and still regularly rely upon, the area of the brain that experiences the world this way. Our present opportunity is to use our relatively new prefrontal cortexes, the parts where executive functioning and higher-order thinking live, to figure out how to stop imagining or exaggerating social threats. Understanding how our own brains are a part of the structural set-up that makes educators vulnerable to BD&E can help us identify and address some of the emotional resistance we experience as we learn to set boundaries.

Not All Boundaries Are Visible

Boundaries can be external and evident to outside observers, or internal, known only to the person who sets and maintains the boundary. The distinction between an internal vs. external boundary is the difference between telling someone about a boundary to vs. enacting a boundary without naming it. You have an internal boundary, for example, around sharing your banking information in casual conversation with new acquaintances.

Internal boundaries often involve shifts in perspective. Changing your thinking from being in relationship to your school district to thinking about your school district like a regulatory agency like the IRS is an example of a shift in perspective that can instate an internal boundary. Once you've shifted your perspective, your boundaries may change automatically or even emerge organically. For example, if you understand that your district is built to be generally extractive, you no longer allow yourself to hope for excellent professional development from the district. When required PD is offered, it's now a pleasant surprise if you learn anything useful at all, instead of being a letdown every time it's predictably terrible.

Do I wish all district PD was life-changingly amazing? Of course! But it's not. It's not fair, it's not right, and it's not worth giving any more energy to complaining about it. And lo, an internal boundary is born.

Boundaries are external when we chose to vocalize them. Externalizing a boundary can help us to maintain it more clearly and easily. My favorite example of an externalized boundary came from Dr. Doris Santoro (coiner of "demoralization"). I was prepping a session with teachers and wanted to use an image from her book, so I emailed her for permission. I received an auto-reply which informed me that she checks email once per work day for an hour, that she doesn't check email after 7 p.m. nor on weekends, and that she'd respond to my email when she got to it based on that schedule.

Mind. Blown.

Dr. Santoro's decision to publicize her boundary may feel risky to someone who has either never seen such a boundary modeled or never been in a context that supports (let alone encourages) such a boundary. As the recipient, because it was a) clear, b) did not attempt to justify the need for the boundary, and c) simply stated facts, it was easy for me to support her boundary without having any feelings about it. In emailing another academic without a self-preserving auto-reply, I may have felt an anxious urge to write again in case my email was lost under too many emails. In this case, it was easy for me to wait a while (a week and a half, which seemed reasonable for a professor to respond to a stranger who wanted something from her for free during the academic year). Dr. Santoro taught me how to treat her. And everybody got what they needed.

Is There Such a Thing as a Negotiable Boundary?

Every boundary-setting adventure is a negotiation. If we are too rigid about boundaries that don't matter that much, we're hard to collaborate with. If we police our boundaries so fiercely that they interfere with our required relationships, that doesn't serve us, either. We do best when we can negotiate win-win situations.

Before you decide if you're going to externalize a boundary, and even before you frame what the boundary is, consider 3 things; the stakes, the rules, and when you'll walk away. You'll determine the stakes when you identify the values that guide your life and practice in Chapter 5. You'll co-author the rules as you begin setting internal and external boundaries, test them, and learn which of them are easy and which are challenging for you to maintain. After a while, ideally on neither your very best nor your very worst day in the classroom, you'll decide when to walk away by evaluating if the rules are fair enough and if you can afford the stakes. If, at that time, the rules aren't fair and the stakes are too high, it's okay. You can go.

Any time we set a boundary, we are, in fact, inviting conflict. What will we do if the boundary isn't respected? If we do nothing when our boundaries are violated, there goes our self-respect and happiness. If we react to every boundary violation as if it is catastrophic, then we set ourselves up to have to quit jobs and relationships nearly every day. The goal is to determine which boundaries can be internal, which need to be external, which are negotiable, and which are not.

Setting Boundaries—A Learnable, but Rarely Taught, Skill

Through no fault of their own, the people and structures in our lives benefit from us not having boundaries or not enforcing the boundaries we say we have. A person without boundaries is always available, always giving, and always a resource. In organizational structures like the American public education system, this describes the ideal employee: perpetually giving, rarely taking. In interpersonal relationships, this can look slightly different, as we can have boundaries around what we're willing to ask of each other as well as what we're willing to offer each other. Combine that with the way helpers —those who's participation is motivated by approval-seeking—are drawn to the profession, and you can see how quickly we can cultivate school cultures in which saying "no" or admitting limitations is risky. It's hard to set and maintain a boundary in a community that isn't made of boundaried constituent members.

Your school is not alone in perpetuating a minimally-boundaried culture. The selfless (and, therefore, boundaryless) educator is a stereotype represented far and wide. Depending upon when you were born, you saw at least one of the following movies celebrating this martyr model of teaching on the big screen: *Stand And Deliver*, *Dead Poets' Society*, or *Freedom Writers*. These productions show world that the best teachers are those who give everything—their marriages, their kitchen tables, their own mental health—to their students and their craft. While I mean no disrespect to Jaime Escalante, Samuel Pickering, and Erin Gruwell, all excellent educators on whose backs the martyr model is perpetuated, we must understand how their stories being the most popular representations of educators is harmful.

We are explicitly taught that developing meaningful teaching expertise requires a rejection of our own needs.

Let's take Erin's *Freedom Writers*, for example. The movie emphasized honoring poor students of color as whole humans with valuable things to say (good), normalized the dissolution of Erin's marriage as an example of martyrdom's expected costs (bad), and minimized the fact that Erin left the classroom after four years (dishonest). Similar to our fascination with tortured artists, somehow we're less allowed to celebrate the tens of thousands of excellent, expert educators who manage to both hold and support lovingly high expectations for their students while also exercising regularly, eating vegetables, and prioritizing their own family lives, at least often enough to continue to have family lives.

Rather than subscribing to the martyr model, it's our obligation to acknowledge that we hurt ourselves, our students, and our profession when we sacrifice our own well-being. This harm is particularly apparent when we overextend ourselves in the name of praise-chasing or in an effort to outrun invisible, imaginary threats to our livelihood.

Setting boundaries is scary. Internally, we fear rejection, that we'll be judged as less valuable or less committed, that we won't be generally loved, or even liked. We aren't structurally supported to do it (cue psychopathic system montage). Because of the first two reasons, we don't have practice in boundary setting. Thankfully, boundary setting is a skill and is therefore something we can learn to identify and strive to improve.

Not ready to set boundaries out of love for yourself ? Improve your boundaries for your students who, by existing, make boundary setting a challenging activity in the first place.

We Can, and Must, Do Hard Things—For Our Students.

From a space and time perspective, it's clear that maintaining boundaries can prevent burnout and exploitation. What's less obvious, but much more important, is that boundary maintenance is essential to preventing demoralization. By aligning our boundaries with the values that brought us into the profession, we can ensure that our time and energy are being spent serving the highest good. When we act in this manner, we're also doing the most essential and least acknowledged part of our job—we're showing students how to be a person.

Teachers play an important role in students' development as humans. In today's United States of America, school-age children will spend most of their waking hours with adults who aren't their primary care-givers. As a social species, we don't just learn from the lectures our teachers offer us; we learn from the way those teachers conduct themselves as humans during every single interaction. If, as an educator, I am stressed and preoccupied but can muster just enough energy to "turn on" a forced pleasantness for the start of a lesson, my students will see that. Without a doubt.

We can never be certain about the lessons that students will extract from our behaviors. Still, it's hard to imagine that many students would conclude that we are a steady source of support if we don't steadily enact supportiveness. If we are authentically available to be pleasant and present because we aren't over-taxed, we're that much more able to interact with ease—and reliability. Heck, we might even be able to field challenging or conflictual moments with curiosity, grace, humor, and a non-defensive commitment to always hold our students' experiences as our sacred privilege to witness and support.

By managing our own stress and availability, we are not only less stressed and more available for our students, but (most importantly) we're modeling for them that this way of being is, indeed, possible.

An oft-referenced quote in the land of boundary building is, "You teach people how to treat you."[24] What's less acknowledged is that, by modeling how we will and will not be treated, we are inadvertently teaching our students about human relationships.

We are modeling for our students that it's both possible and okay to expect to be treated as a whole and sacred human.

It's here, in modeling how to be a person, that boundary maintenance can protect us from demoralization. Because the values that draw us to the profession tend to be relate to the growth and development of the students we support (and relate less, say, to proficiency percentages end-of-level exams), our responsibility in modeling those values is evident. For example, even if my practice is motivated by my desire to help students to become lifelong learners, I'm likely to behave in opposition to that value if I'm too exhausted to model curiosity for my students in our day-to-day interactions. If I want them to be resilient problem solvers, but all I model is giving my time, brain space, and power away to tasks and obligations that deplete me, I'm not modeling resilient problem solving. If I want to build a compassionate citizenry but am so exhausted that I meet student requests with sharpness and sarcasm, I'm behaving in stark opposition to my values. Not only does this do harm to my students, but it fast tracks me towards a self-inflicted demoralization.

Measure Boundary Effectiveness in Units of Resentment

It's tempting to think that the teachers who say no to everything (literally everything), who arrive at the contract day's start and leave as soon as contractually allowed, who don't take work home, and who lower their expectations for their students to make their own jobs easier are the ones who have the best boundaries. False. These are not boundaries. This is abandonment. They are leaving the building, figuratively and physically.

Generally, while reactionary, rigid behaviors technically prevent gross exploitation with respect to time, they actually increase burnout and demoralization because in them, the practitioner is relating to the work itself as toxic. Instead of these kinds of boundaries preventing resentment, these

---

[24] Attributed both to Phil McGraw and Tony Gaskins. The complete quote states: "You teach people how to treat you by what you allow, what you stop, and what you reinforce."

approaches assume that the only relationship we can have with work is one of resentment, and so we'd better limit our interactions with our obligations. While we can have compassion for colleagues stuck in rigid work rejection, we can also reframe resentment to better empower ourselves.

Your resentment is your most valuable guide in your teaching practice. Resentment will show up when you haven't honored a boundary. Sometimes you'll discover a boundary that you didn't even know you had because you'll notice you're feeling resentful before you even knew you needed a boundary.

As helpers, we often commit to things via a secret contract. In return, as part of this contract that only we know about, we may be expecting something as non-transactional as gratitude or appreciation, or as concrete as expecting our colleague to cover one class for us for every time we cover for them. When our expectations aren't met, we feel resentment. Rather than aiming that resentment at the people or situations that didn't deliver on the unspoken contract, we can learn from it. If, moving forward, you are able to make your expectations clearer, you may be able to participate without being harmed in the future. If the things you need in return aren't things you feel comfortable explicitly asking for, that's a clear sign that your energy and intentions can't afford to make that commitment.

Want to do Good? Admit That You're on Your Own.

As educators are compulsively collaborative—at first. The practitioners you know who are salty, dismissive, and straight-up grouchy? They most likely started their careers with hearts in their eyes and hopes in their hearts about how supported they would be by their colleagues, their schools, their districts, their states, and even federal policy. Before they got resentful.

In writing this chapter, I explored many situations from my teaching past and held them up against the "resentment test." To my surprise, the one that stood out wasn't dramatic, egregious, nor illegal. It was quiet. Personal. And painful. I was in the office shortly after the school day had adjourned, finishing up some transportation paperwork for a field trip from which we had just returned. One of the parents who had kindly volunteered during the fieldtrip approached me. "You know what you should do?" she asked, "You should apply for a grant to have a community garden at the school."

My inner rage was immediate and complete. Thank goodness I had a form to pretend to be focused on. I replied with something pleasantly dismissive enough that she didn't complain about me to the principal (win). And I learned some things, both about myself and about the profession.

If I had reacted, unfiltered, to that well-meaning mom's earnest suggestion about a lovely idea that would certainly have enriched the school, I would have done so by listing:

- How sprawling the state content expectations are
- How wildly variable student experiences, capacities, and availabilities are (which is not a barrier, but which does require meticulous, differentiated planning and a deep quiver of instructional approaches to support, all of which take time and energy)
- How lucky she is to have her child in my class, where I was willing to to submit a "plan to plan" application for field trips a year before the trip itself, and then wade, uncompensated, through the red tape and risk to build meaningful field trips once per quarter
- All of the grants and partnerships and fundraisers and program collaborations I had already initiated towards authentically engaging and supporting my students
- Any other nitpicky thing I could list about either a) how hard the job is, b) how good I am at it, or c) how underappreciated I am

I learned two things during that conversation: First, I don't do great when people begin sentences with, "You should..." and second, I would never get the recognition I had so humbly made my condition for signing on to this extremely tough job. I'll state that second one again because it is the hardest truth about why we, as practitioners, have to cultivate and enforce our own boundaries with uncompromising commitment:

You will never get the recognition you deserve.

Even in a world where educators are universally esteemed (which is not, unfortunately, our world), there is no way for anyone to fully know what you do, so there's no way for anyone to fully appreciate it. We'll never know how many times you bite your tongue to keep instruction headed in the right direction, read the room correctly, or try a risky-but-exactly-right strategy. We won't see the hundreds of thousands of decisions you make every week to keep your classrooms humming and your students cared for and comfortable enough to take learning risks. We'll miss out on getting weepy at the perfectly worded praise you offer, the sensitivity you bring to bear as you build challenging instruction that still supports students to experience success. Because what you do is so complex, we simply can't see it all. Even if we try.

I am so sorry to be the bearer of this news, but there's no way around it. You will never be fully appreciated to even a fraction of the level that you deserve. It's not fair, and it's not right. It's just true. So, knowing this, you get to make a decision. You can either slide into a lifetime of resentment over an unattainable boundary, or you can acknowledge that you'll never get what you deserve externally and figure out a way to be okay internally, anyway. If total and fair recognition is a requirement for you to avoid feeling resentful, it's possible there are not enough boundaries in the universe that ensure that you get the appreciation you deserve. Like acknowledging a psychopathic system to support your own sanity, it's also important to name the ways in which "protecting yourself" with boundaries may be an impossibility. If this proves true for you, it's okay for you to be done.

There's no right or wrong choice in the way you approach your boundary development. And there's no judgment. Perhaps you take a hard look at what you're putting into your practice vs. what you're getting out and are forced to acknowledge that teaching may be too expensive for you. That's okay. You may, however, be able to arm yourself ahead of time with the ideas, skills, and approaches in the following chapters (and the thousands of practice hacks you'll discover and invent along your journey) and figure out a way to enjoy the heck out of your life's work—even if you're never recognized for it.

Too Long, Didn't Read
Chapter 4:
Boundaries Are Necessary and Nurturing

Ideas

- Boundaries are scary because we are a social species with millennia of evolutionary pressure causing us to worry about what other people think (being kicked out of the group meant almost certain death).
- Not all boundaries are visible. Boundaries don't necessarily need to be publicly broadcast in order to be impactful.
  Internal shifts in how we define relationships can help us manage our asks and offers, thereby managing our overextension and our disappointment.
- Setting boundaries is a skill, and we can improve.
- Setting and maintaining good boundaries helps our students in two ways; it helps us to be available for them in healthy ways, and it models what it looks like to set healthy boundaries.

Strategies

- Re-define your relationship to your school district by acknowledging it's designed to function more like the IRS than a system meant to support your personal growth and wellbeing.
- Scan for resentment. When you find some, look to see where you need a boundary.
- Practice setting and maintaining both internal and external boundaries, particularly before you quit teaching entirely. Learning this skill can be game-changing, and career-saving, for suffering educators.

Chapter 5

Reclaim Self-Care, Reclaim Your Self

In which we explore how the idea of self-care has been used against educators and how you can figure out who you are, what you need, and what you care about to strategically care for yourself, anyway.

"Figure out who you are and do it on purpose."
— Dolly Parton —

"If you get tired, learn to rest. Not to quit."
— Banksy —

We Must Reclaim Self-Care

"Self-care" is all the rage these days. A cursory social media scroll would have us believe that self-care means spending time in luxurious destinations, ideally involving a body of water. Or fingernail maintenance. Or a face mask.[25] But it definitely means spending money and feeling good.

Let's explore the intention motivating self-care initiatives along with definitions of self-care, itself. A school district might, define self-care as squeezing in some meditation on our lunch break, or holding contests about drinking more water. Drinking water and meditating are fine, we aren't critiquing the activities. What's critique-able is district intention to deploy self-care strategies to increase educator resilience in place of meaningful policy change. Districts use self-care initiatives to appear caring while

---

[25] Teaching, like nursing, is a feminized profession. Self-care has also been feminized. This is a bummer for two reasons. First, this alignment betrays the scale at which the system is ready to assign individual responsibility to systemic overwork. Second, it reveals one of the ways that patriarchy hurts men; when we feminize self-care so that women have to care themselves out of their structurally caused pain, we feminize the very idea of self-care. In so doing, we deny masculine people socially acceptable avenues of self-care.

continuing to over-work and undervalue you.

Educators need to reclaim self-care from district and school involvement because it's not the state's business to manage your self-care. It's the state's business to build structures, policies, and procedures that minimize the demand for the need for extreme self-care in the first place. Unfortunately, for reasons we'll explore in Chapter 6, the state is incentivized to keep you exhausted and minimally able to participate. Districts offering self-care support without making substantive structural changes to your work load is gaslighting.

Self-care conversations often invoke aircraft emergency instructions to "put on your own oxygen mask first." Unfortunately, people misinterpret this to mean that, once your metaphorical oxygen mask is on, your work is done. We see rich White women confirm from their yoga mats that all they can do is care for themselves. So that's literally all they do. In this frame, self-care is a proxy for a pull-yourself-up-by-your-bootstraps stance claiming that, if someone can't access certain types of self-care which cost both time and money, they just don't want it enough. The "all I can do is care for myself" stance is also a coping conclusion in response to broader cultural burnout. We say we can only be responsible for ourselves when we're too overwhelmed to attend a community council meeting or learn about an issue that our community faces but that doesn't directly affect us.

There is nothing wrong with water-adjacent vacations, meditating yoga, or buying stuff. The bummer about self-care being coopted by consumerism, individualism, and employee productivity, however, is that "self-care" in these contexts contains neither true self nor true care.

> For self-care to become meaningful for educators,
> we have to reclaim the self and re-define care.

Thankfully, we aren't the first to walk this road, and we aren't alone.

The term "self-care" became broadly aligned with how we'll use it in the 1960s and '70s. Back then, it had nothing to do with bubble baths; self-care was a term used by Black Panther organizers building community clinics in response to a lack of basic health services and dangerous medical discrimination. The "self" in the Black Panther model was the community. The "care" in the Black Panther model was essential, basic medical care requisite for people to function and participate in their communities.[26]

As educators, we share some goals and constraints with the community-centric organizers of the Black Panther Party—and we have a lot to learn from them. We are similar in that wish to serve our own communities, and we are not sufficiently cared for by the structures we're acting within to be automatically well-supported do that work. We can learn how to enact self-care in a way that supports our ongoing ability to participate, not as an excuse to permanently withdraw. In order to use self-care for community good, we need to be honest about exactly what parts of ourselves need exactly what type of care. Skipping out on participating in our worlds is not self-care. Building your life around meaningful self-care so that you can participate more fully is the goal. We understand that we strive to put the oxygen mask on ourselves precisely so that we can re-engage, precisely so that we can help others secure their own safety and well-being.

We can find ideas supporting community-serving self-care as far back as we have records of people being people. The world's contemplative, religious, and philosophical institutions revolve around this very question;

What type of self shall I cultivate to support good in the world?

Usually, the answer doesn't involve buying something from Gwyneth Paltrow. Rather, "[s]elf-care isn't performative self-coddling. It's doing the hard work of examining and improving yourself in order to better serve the world."[27] And without sacrificing yourself in a manner that you can no longer contribute at all.

Know Yourself

Now that we've confirmed that no one will be throwing you parades nor offering you life-changing amounts of money for your dedication to your classroom (sad face), we can commit to the idea that you, and only you, are going to care for yourself. To do that well, you must know who you are.

You've already started; you knew yourself well enough to pick up this book. While you'll continue this work in the following activities, you'll also continue long after these activities are complete.

---

[26] Nelson, A. (2011). Body and soul: The Black Panther Party and the fight against medical discrimination. U of Minnesota Press.

[27] Taylor, C. (2019, September). You've been getting self-care all wrong. It's a political act and always has been. Mashable. Retrieved from www.mashable.com

ACTIVITY: Self-Knowledge—Part 1

Grab a piece of scratch paper and separate it into seven columns, labeling the first column "Stuff I Like to Do," like so:

Stuff I like to do						

Under the "Stuff I Like to Do" column, list things you like to do in your spare time. Be real about who you are and what makes you happy. Treat it like a brainstorm; get every idea possible joy-making thing you can think of on your list. Include consensual R- & X-rated activities, as well as controlled substance. This list is yours, and no one else needs to see it. The longer you have been teaching, the harder it may be to generate a list of things that bring you joy. This is normal, and important to name as you work to re-build a rich, full life.

Now imagine that it's spring break, the house is clean, and all kids, pets, and other dependents are taken care of. What would you add to the list?

Now imagine that it's summer, your grades are done, your first month of instruction for fall is already planned, and you found a free $500 cash in the gutter that the cops said you could keep. What would you add to the list?

Hold on to your list. We'll learn more and come back to it.

Not All Activities Are Equal—Caring vs. Coping

Self-care is frequently misunderstood to mean "stuff that feels good." Is it important to feel good? Yes. Are all forms of feeling good created equal? No way. That difference is the difference between caring and coping.

When my BD&E was so all-consuming that I was no longer behaving honorably nor joyfully, my internal dialogue changed. After an exhausting day, I identified with the exhaustion I felt so fully that I would let myself off the Inner Adult hook. I said things to myself like, "Today was too much. I have nothing left to give. There is no way I can exercise." I felt victimized, but I hadn't named the sources of my victimization in order to disempower them. Instead, I started acting like a victim.

At a certain point, the conversation in my head stopped entirely. It just became a decision that my dopamine-seeking brain seemed to make without me. I'd reach past the vegetables for the pasta. I'd let one beer turn into four. I'd watch TV. And keep watching. I *couldn't* do anything else. All of it was to numb against the combo of dread and anxiety that I was carrying around everywhere I went. All I wanted was to not feel those feelings anymore. Rather than exploring my feelings and changing how I interacted with them, I was simply striving to not feel them. To be numb. To excuse myself from participating in the life I had chosen so decisively.

It is risky to publicly acknowledge my stress and my socially judged coping mechanisms. I have been saddened by how my honesty here has impacted some friendships, and how people view me as a person. Still, transparency is important. Education ranks among the top 10 professions likely to struggle with "problem drinking."[28] I use alcohol-related examples intentionally, as I have seen alcohol use be tightly correlated with BD&E in myself and my colleagues.

While drinking is a commonly understood mechanism for addictive behavior, it's not the only one. Anything that brings us short-term relief has the potential to bring us long-term pain. We can be addicted to so many things. You are the only one who can decide if a behavior is a problem for you.

---

[28] American Addiction Centers. (2023, January 19). Professions with the highest rates of alcohol abuse. Alcohol.org. Retrieved March 1, 2023, from https://alcohol.org/professions/

The Difference Between Caring and Coping is How it Feels When You're Done

Both coping and caring feel good at some point. Coping stops feeling good the second I stop the coping behavior. If I'm coping, I'm pushing a pause button on whatever emotion I'm trying not to feel, whatever conflict or pressure-filled expectation I'm avoiding. Coping behaviors do, indeed, provide relief from these feelings. Temporarily. When they stop, though— when the bottle is empty, the series is over, the party ends (literally or figuratively)—all of those feelings are sitting there waiting for us, unchanged. Coping feels good while it's happening. That's why we do it. Too much coping, though, and we start to inadvertently multiply the parts of our life we feel we need to cope about, and a cycle can emerge. The cycle or coping initiating more need to cope is as exhausting as it is predictable.

Self-care can, like coping, feel good while we're engaging in it, but it doesn't have to. We know it's self-care if we feel better, if we are better, or if our world is better because we've engaged in it, either on a short- or long-term scale (but, ideally, both).

ACTIVITY: Self-Knowledge—Part 2 (Coping vs. Caring)

Find your paper with your "Stuff I Like to Do" table. Name the second column from the left "Coping or Caring?"

Stuff I like to do	Coping or Caring?				

Next, categorize each of the activities you've listed in your "Stuff I Like to Do" column into either "coping" or "caring" activities. Use the definition of "coping" and the definition of "self-care" above to distinguish between the list of your favorite activities, keeping two things in mind. First, the same activity may be coping under certain conditions and caring under others. For example, sufficient exercise for healthy brain chemistry is a caring behavior, and excessive exercise to justify procrastination is coping. Second, individual context matters. For example, one educator may feel like drinking alone is a bad, but a drink with friends is an intentional caring activity, while another might feel like social drinking is a coping tool for social anxiety.

Self-Care Requires Showing Up

Now that you're clear on the difference between coping and caring, you're ready to take a look at some of the patterns that can get educators in trouble. In the early stages of self-care awareness, people can allow their Inner Child to dominate decisions, and so-called "self-care" can be coping-heavy. Let's use the coping vs. caring filter to run through a few potential scenarios so that you can see how sneaky this stuff is. We want to side-step the victimhood that accompanies identification with the martyr model of teaching. Instead, the goal is to fully step into our authentic, additive, enriching, Inner-Adult-driven self-care.

It's tempting to skip boring meetings, required classes, and anything that falls outside of our contracted teaching schedule. However, bailing on our basic contractual obligations is a very different choice than limiting the number of optional external commitments we make. In most cases, once you've made a commitment, the Adult stance is to honor it.

If I start letting myself off the hook from my obligations because "I don't feel like it," my Inner Child is clearly in the driver's seat. My Inner Child tempts me to do things like fib about feeling sick or having a flat tire. The trouble is, it actually takes more energy to skip out on our commitments than it does to follow through with them. If I fib, I need to remember which lies I told to whom. I need to follow up to see if I missed anything important (because even the most frustrating meetings and classes contain some important information, even if it's just the knowledge that you didn't miss anything important). Worse, when I inevitably actually am sick or actually have a flat tire, I've already used my excuse. Now I have the additional stress of worrying about what my colleagues or administrators think about my messiness on top of fixing a flat while I'm sick with a fever (likely in the rain because that's how things tend to happen...).

There will be times when you want to skip an obligation. How will you know if it's worth it? If it's an Inner Child decision vs. an Inner Adult one? You'll run it through the same "coping vs. caring" filter by asking yourself if you'll be better off in all areas of life, including your practice, if you bail on your obligation.

Self-Care, Like Teaching, is a Practice

At this point, you're likely picking up that self-care isn't all bubble baths and happy hours. Rather, self-care is a discipline. There's a tight correlation between how effective our self-care is and how developed our Inner Adult is. If you haven't had many models for how to care for yourself, and you've swung wildly between Inner Parent over-responsibility and Inner Child tantrum-y rejections of responsibility in exchange for activities that hurt you in the long run, building a self-care plan can feel overwhelming.

Good news! You have what you need to build a self-care plan that's perfectly tailored toward your unique you-ness. What's more, with time, you'll get better and better at it. You'll also have some days that are better than others, so it won't be perfectly linear growth, but with intention and attention, you will get better at caring for yourself.

Self-care can be categorized based on different areas of our lives: environmental, occupational, financial, intellectual, physical, social, emotional, and spiritual.[29] While all of these components are essential to a healthy, sane, situated life, there are areas over which an individual educator may have less daily control (environmental and occupational) or which deserve their own book (financial). For our purposes of daily, strategic self-care planning, we'll focus on the most immediate five key self-care categories: intellectual, physical, social, emotional, and spiritual. Your whole self deserves care in all 8 areas. As you get great at caring for yourself in your immediate world, addressing care at larger scales can become more and more possible.

Here's more about the five we will focus on in this book:

---

[29] Swarbrick, M. (2006). A Wellness Approach. Psychiatric Rehabilitation Journal, 29(4), 311–314.

Intellectual Self-Care

Practicing intellectual self-care impacts our prefrontal cortex: the part of our brain that understands deep time, selects our values, and understands, at least cognitively, that one day we're going to perish. These care practices include creativity, generativity, and risk-taking. Intellectual engagement is a given for teachers—at least until we're teaching the same content to the same demographic group of students in the same way.

Engaging in intellectual self-care keeps you connected to your Inner Child, as it's the home of wonder and awe in us (shared with spiritual self-care, of course). Attending to diversity in intellectual self-care can protect against BD&E. Even if your job challenges you, consider seeking opportunities to learn and grow that relate to your interests and abilities outside of the classroom.

Physical Self-Care

Acknowledging that we have bodies and that the state of our bodies impacts our ability to regulate stress is essential. Physical self-care keeps our prefrontal cortexes available for the kinds of interactions we want to have with our students and within our personal relationships.

Physical self-care practices don't require athletic ability or gym memberships. Essential components include diet, exercise, and sleep hygiene (more in Chapter 10). Regarding diet, figure out what works for you. I like Michael Pollen's suggestion to "[e]at food, not too much, mostly plants."[30] Exercise can be impactful in a self-care frame even on the tiniest scale, like shoulder shrugs during passing periods, calf stretches while we wait for the copy machine, and breathing deeply while we're taking attendance. Anything we can do to stay present with our bodies when we experience stress will help to lower our stress response. We need a bare minimum of 30 minutes of elevating our heart rate three times per week to get all of those gnarly stress hormones out of our bloodstream. [31]

---

[30] Pollan, M. (2008). In defense of food: An eater's manifesto. Penguin.

[31] Jackson, E. M. (2013). Stress relief: The role of exercise in stress management. ACSM's Health & Fitness Journal, 17(3), 14-19.

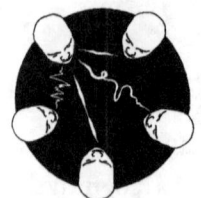

Social Self-Care

By my estimate, 80% of educators are introverts. While extroverts are refueled by spending time with people, social interaction drains introverts. To care for yourself socially, be honest about your social appetite and honor it. Select your companionship intentionally and strategically. For example, rather than committing to meeting a friend at a work party which you're 90% likely to bail on ten minutes before it starts, allow yourself to attend the activities and social interactions you enjoy. Say 'no' to invitations that are too expensive for you from a social energy standpoint. And don't worry about explaining.

Figure out who your friends are and act like it. Remember how we started this adventure by acknowledging that you're going to die? Who would you regret not spending more time with? That list is where you invest the social energy you have available outside of school.

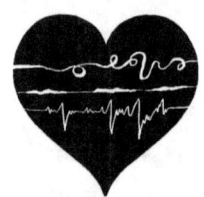

Emotional Self-Care

When we feel our feelings without judgment, fear, impatience, nor critique, we are practicing emotional self-care. Emotional self-care can be practiced alone or with company. We practice emotional self-care whenever we're processing our own feelings. Watching a sad movie and crying about a tragic wombat attack only counts as emotional self-care if you had a tragic wombat experience, and the movie is helping you to feel your own precise feelings more deeply.

When we don't allow ourselves to feel our feelings, they come out sideways, either as different feelings or as mental or physical symptoms. If you are more angry, irritable, forgetful, anxious, or depressed than usual, may be because you aren't allowing yourself to fully feel the range of emotions one regularly encounters in the course of a day in the classroom. Strategies for feeling your feelings can include chatting with a trusted friend, partner, or confidant (animal companions count), journaling, making stuff with your hands—as long as you're intentionally saying, "I feel (insert emotion here)."

Spiritual Self-Care

People of faith, agnostics, and atheists alike need to practice spiritual self-care. If that title doesn't work for this category, you can call it "Connecting To Something More Meaningful Than Myself."

This can get tricky for those of us who feel like teaching is our life's purpose, the reason we're on the planet, our calling, or any other connection to significance and meaning-making. It's great that you find your work meaningful, but you're going to need to pick another one. You need another focal meaning-maker because you need something to hold on to when your essential, deeply meaningful work in the classroom has days that feel meaningless.

Spiritual self-care may not require a new hobby or cause. It may be as simple as pausing to appreciate the day (gratitude practices are ubiquitous, time-tested via contemplative and monastic traditions the world over, and demonstrably effective). But something's got to matter more than you do.

ACTIVITY: Self-Knowledge—Part 3

Return to your "Stuff I like to Do" table again. Label the remaining five columns with the five components of a self-care plan.

Stuff I like to do	Coping or Caring?	Intellectual	Social	Physical	Emotional	Spiritual

Read through your list, and for every activity you listed, check the self-care categories honored by that activity. For example, if I do the crossword with my cousin every Sunday, I check the intellectual and social columns. Going for a hike with my book club friends gets me a check in the intellectual, social, and physical columns, but also emotional (because we're good enough friends to talk about real stuff) and spiritual (because being outside helps me connect with something bigger than myself).

As you evaluate each activity, you'll notice that some have higher values than others, and some activities have different values when enacted differently. If I can choose between watching crappy TV alone on the couch (coping), while exercising (caring: physical), or with my friend while exercising and we can connect about finding fascination with the show (caring: physical, social), then I can choose to engage intentionally toward being more caring over time.

Some activities are higher-value than others, meaning they involve more checkmarks in more columns. I can go the gym and watch crappy TV with my friend (caring: physical, social), or I could go for a walk outside with that same friend (caring: physical, social, and emotional because I feel freer to talk privately, spiritual because I connect to a sense of meaning greater than myself when I'm outside).

Of course, all of these examples are only examples. You get to build your list that's right for you, and you get to determine which activities satisfy which self-care categories. The goal here is to notice that some activities are much higher-value from a self-care perspective than others. Once you start noticing this, you can start to increase the effectiveness of your self-care strategy by raising the value of your activities so that they include as many categories as possible.

Venting Is Coping, Not Caring

Venting is a time-honored practice among teachers. Biologically speaking, this makes sense—if we're solely considering our mammalian brain, and if we let what we want in the moment override what we want most.

Venting is arguing without the other party present. This is an addictive behavior; it feels really good to vent, because when we're arguing with someone who isn't there, we always win. Our brains get the same happy-chemical dose we would have gotten from actually "winning." Our lives, however, haven't actually changed in any way, and we're left needing to deal with the same disappointments that drove us to venting in the first place. And so, we vent. And the coping cycle continues.

Friendships forged in mutual commitments to allow each other to complain can fall short of hitting the social self-care mark. If my relationship is built on frequent vocalization of helplessness and negativity, it's unlikely that the friendship is helping me to learn about myself and grow. I might not even feel that safe or supported; if my relationship is predicated on venting because "we're always right," then it might not be safe for me when I am inevitably wrong about something.

Venting counts as coping because, when we're done engaging in it, our world remains the same. Venting contributes to intrapersonal oppression because it can spread a sense of powerlessness. Altering our approach to venting is an excellent way to cultivate some serious Inner Adult strength.

To move from venting-as-coping into discussion-as-caring, we can make a few easy shifts. These shifts can not only support less venting and more acting to better our situations, they can also better our friendships, which are allowed to move to more positive, authentically supportive places.

Here are some easy ways to shift venting conversations into more worthwhile, caring, and enriching discussions:

- Notice when you're tempted to vent, and instead of launching into a complaint, start the conversation by asking for what you're craving. For example, start with, "I'm feeling really frustrated. Can I ask you for some validation?"
- If you notice you're tempted to ask for validation a lot, consider asking about things happening in your friend's life, instead. If a part of us that believes we aren't good enough is activated, no amount of being told we're good enough is going to change our minds. It may, however, change our relationships, and not always for the better.
- Request specific feedback. You might strategize to build a meeting agenda or share a draft of an email before you send it to an administrator. The more specific you can be about the feedback you'd like, the better. For example, "I'm hoping for a warm but professional tone in this email. Does that come across to you?"
- When a friend approaches you hoping to vent, help nudge the conversation towards something actionable. You might ask questions like, "How can I best support you in this situation?" or "It seems like you've been really bothered by this. Want to brainstorm things you could do to deal with it in a way that works for you?"

Your Practice, and Your Life, Are Values-Motivated

If we acknowledge that the #1 regret expressed by those reflecting on their lives is, "I wish I had the courage to live a life true to myself, not the life others expected of me," then it follows that we need to figure out how to live lives true to ourselves, which requires us to know ourselves. Knowing one's self isn't a finite adventure; it's not like one day you didn't know yourself, and then the next day you did. Your "self" isn't a declarative fact you can google or keep in your back pocket for trivia night. Rather, knowing one's self is an ongoing investigation.

Teaching invites constant self-discovery through curiosity about our motivations, choices, and reactions.

Compared to teachers, people with desk jobs get thousands fewer opportunities to explore who they are, who they want to be, and how to behave in ways that get those two in better alignment. A teaching practice is a perpetual invitation to extreme self-awareness. Or it can be, at least, if we actively choose to engage with it that way.

One way to know ourselves is to understand what we value. Of course, our values will likely shift at different times in life and in different professional and social contexts. No need to claim your values as a promise to keep. Instead, the goal is to acknowledge that our values, like our practices, are ever-shifting, and that even our ever-shifting practices are always motivated by our currently-held values.

Suppose your practice isn't motivated by your values, particularly because you haven't yet figured out precisely what yours are. In that case, it will be motivated by the default values of the system. For example, I have yet to work with an educator who embraces irritability, compliance, and data manipulation as the values they want to guide their classroom. Yet, I've worked with many educators whose on-the-ground practice enacts values like these before, and at the expense of, any others.

Know Your Values

Following this paragraph, you'll find a list of values.[32] This list is a good start, but it certainly doesn't include every possible value every human could hold. If, at any point during this next activity (or in life, ever), you identify a value that's important to you that isn't represented on this list, please add it.

ACTIVITY: Values Exercise

Identify your (shifting) values. If you're okay with writing in books, mark each set of values with the corresponding symbol here. If you'd rather not write in this book, you can journal or grab a piece of scratch paper.

Note your top three values for each of the following questions:

Symbol	Identify three values for each of the following questions:
●	What values defined your family's relationship to work?
★	What values were prominent in how you thought and acted as a student? (imagine yourself at the age of the students you teach)
✓	What values drew you to teaching as a profession?
✗	What values is your current teaching practice enacting?
☺	What values do you WANT to define your teaching practice?

Care for Your Values

After identifying the three values that you want to define your teaching practice, commit to them. Do this in whatever way works for your style. Keep them on a sticky note on your laptop. Say them in a revolving mantra in quiet meditation to yourself for three minutes before you start working on planning or before you begin your day. Identify images and objects that remind you of your values and populate your classroom with them. Consider starting your day with a journaling activity in which you envision enacting each value or closing the work day by noting where your values showed up in your practice that day. I'd almost go so far as to suggest a tattoo of your values, except that they may grow and change as you do; if you're okay with your tattoo being a snapshot of you during a particular time in the development of your practice, go for it.

---

[32] List adapted from one of Scott Jeffrey's as a part of his professional coaching practice CEOsage.

Acceptance	Contribution	Foresight
Accomplishment	Control	Fortitude
Accountability	Conviction	Freedom
Accuracy	Cooperation	Friendship
Achievement	Courage	Fun
Adaptability	Creativity	Generosity
Alertness	Credibility	Genius
Altruism	Curiosity	Goodness
Ambition	Decisiveness	Grace
Amusement	Dedication	Gratitude
Assertiveness	Dependability	Greatness
Authenticity	Determination	Growth
Awareness	Development	Happiness
Balance	Devotion	Hard work
Beauty	Dignity	Harmony
Boldness	Discipline	Health
Bravery	Discovery	Honesty
Brilliance	Drive	Honor
Calm	Effectiveness	Hope
Candor	Efficiency	Humility
Capacity	Empathy	Humor
Caution	Emotion	Imagination
Certainty	Empowerment	Improvement
Challenge	Endurance	Independence
Charity	Energy	Individuality
Clarity	Enjoyment	Innovation
Cleverness	Enthusiasm	Insightfulness
Comfort	Equality	Inspiration
Commitment	Ethics	Integrity
Communication	Excellence	Intelligence
Community	Experience	Intensity
Compassion	Exploration	Intuition
Competence	Expression	Joy
Concentration	Fairness	Justice
Confidence	Faith	Kindness
Connection	Family	Knowledge
Consciousness	Fame	Lawfulness
Consistency	Fearlessness	Leadership
Contentment	Focus	Learning

Liberty	Reason	Strength
Logic	Recognition	Structure
Love	Reflection	Success
Loyalty	Relationships	Support
Mastery	Respect	Sustainability
Maturity	Responsibility	Teamwork
Meaning	Results	Temperance
Motivation	Reverence	Thoroughness
Openness	Risk	Thoughtfulness
Optimism	Satisfaction	Timeliness
Organization	Security	Tolerance
Originality	Self-reliance	Toughness
Passion	Selflessness	Tranquility
Patience	Sensitivity	Transparency
Peace	Serenity	Trust
Performance	Service	Trustworthiness
Persistence	Sharing	Truth
Playfulness	Significance	Understanding
Poise	Silence	Uniqueness
Potential	Simplicity	Unity
Power	Sincerity	Valor
Presentness	Skillfulness	Vigor
Productivity	Solitude	Vision
Professionalism	Spirituality	Vitality
Prosperity	Spontaneity	Wealth
Purpose	Stability	Winning
Quality	Status	Wisdom
Realism	Stewardship	Wonder

Know Your Parts

We can identify and recite or post sticky notes or tattoo our values all day long, but if we over-identify with the parts of us that encourage us to buy into the martyr model of teaching, we're unlikely to be able to enact our values. What's more, if we super-over-identify, then even examining the parts that make martyrdom appealing can feel like a threat to who we are. This is one of the reasons some educators stick around even though they are clearly suffering deeply from BD&E.

If we're able to name the parts of ourselves that keep us in the gig in unhealthy ways, if we can recognize them as just that—parts. They neither define nor entirely compose us. From this vantage, it's easier for us to look at how our parts are impacting our practice. More importantly, once we've looked at those impacts, we can start inviting some shifts.

The leading expert on "parts work" is Dr. Richard Swartz, whose Internal Family Systems (IFS) model posits that all of us have a bunch of parts inside, and that becoming lovingly acquainted with those parts is the way we develop an Inner Adult. We know we're doing it, Dr. Schwartz contends, when we're cultivating what he calls "the IFS eight Cs: "creativity, courage, curiosity, a sense of connection, compassion, clarity, calm, and confidence."[33]

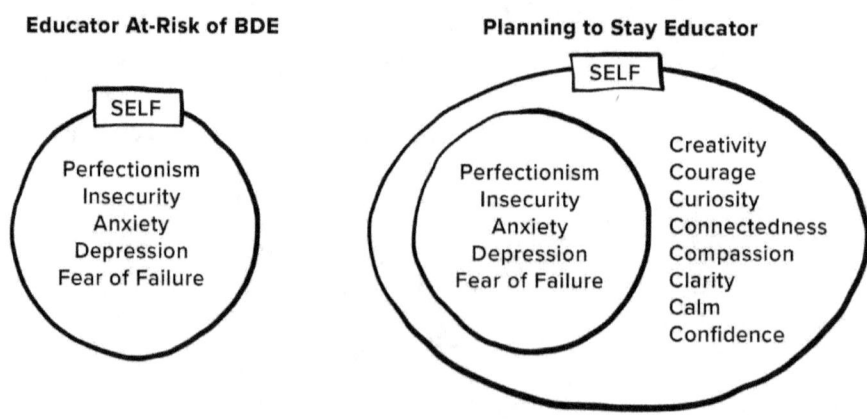

Educator At-Risk of BDE	Planning to Stay Educator
SELF	SELF
Perfectionism Insecurity Anxiety Depression Fear of Failure	Perfectionism Insecurity Anxiety Depression Fear of Failure · Creativity Courage Curiosity Connectedness Compassion Clarity Calm Confidence

---

[33] Schwartz, R. C. (2021). No bad parts: healing trauma and restoring wholeness with the internal family systems model. Sounds True.

If you're planning to stay, you're being honest with yourself about the parts you've got. You're also honoring who you're striving to become.

The example educator is only that—an example. It's important to acknowledge that it can be the same educator as "before and after," or represent two different people.

All kinds of internal components might make us more vulnerable to BD&E: people-pleasing, rebelliousness, a desire to matter and to make a difference, a sense of accountability, guilt, shame, fear, hurt—you name it. Your opportunity is to do some exploration. What are your parts? How do they show up in your practice? What will you need to do to buckle them into the back seat, reclaim your driver's seat as your Inner Adult, and insist on building yourself a practice which allows you to cultivate creativity, courage, curiosity, a sense of connection, compassion, clarity, calm, and confidence?

Too Long; Didn't Read
Chapter 5:
Self-Care Requires Self-Knowledge.

Ideas

- Coping activities stop discomfort momentarily. When we are done with a coping behavior, the world, and our feelings, are the same as when we started (for example: watching TV or drinking alcohol).
- Caring behaviors shift something in us so we, our world, or both are different after having engaged in them (for example: exercising or connecting with a friend)
- Areas of self-care we can impact daily include:
  - Intellectual - caring for our brain with challenge and newness
  - Physical - acknowledging we have a body by moving, drinking water, and eating and sleeping well
  - Social - connecting with people who care about and support us, and who we care about and support (who aren't students)
  - Emotional - naming and feeling our feelings
  - Spiritual - connecting to something more meaningful than ourselves
- Naming your values can protect you against demoralization.
- We are more than our sadness, anxiety, and anger. Cultivating "the 8 C's" (creativity, courage, curiosity, a sense of connection, compassion, clarity, calm, and confidence) can support more present and pleasant versions of ourselves in our classrooms and lives.

Strategies

- Evaluate the way you spend your non-teaching time for coping vs. caring activities.
- Identify "high value" caring activities that involve two or more self-care categories (for example, listening to a new album with a friend may be intellectual and social), or brainstorm ways to create some.
- Name your values, particularly the values that you'd like to define your teaching practice.
- Name the parts of yourself that are impacted negatively by your practice, and consider how cultivating the 8 C's (creativity, courage, curiosity, a sense of connection, compassion, clarity, calm, and confidence) could support those parts to be less impacted.

Chapter 6

Maslow's Hierarchy Missed the Point

In which we explore the structural causes of burnout, demoralization, and exploitation (BD&E), and where we explore how well-meaning educators are tricked into enacting values opposite to the values that brought them to the profession in the first place.

"It is certain, in any case, that ignorance, allied with power,
is the most ferocious enemy justice can have."
— James Baldwin —

"Schools are reflections of the society that designs them."
— Dr. Bryan A. Brown —[34]

Timing Matters

If you read this book during the school year and need concrete, specific strategies to improve your experience immediately, you may want to skip to the second section. No worries! That's okay. You know best what you need.

Building a deep structural understanding of the ideological and institutional causes of your burnout, demoralization, and exploitation might be more approachable in a loungey, bare-foot-in-the-grass moment than a how-do-I-make-tomorrow-happen moment. If now is not the time for this chapter, just as you've learned to calendar your priorities in other areas of your life, make a note on the calendar to return to it sometime in July.

---

[34] Brown, B. A. (2021). Science in the city: Culturally relevant STEM education. Harvard Education Press. 18.

Every System Is Perfectly Designed to Get the Results It Gets

Often, practitioners come to the classroom from one of two experiences; we either liked school or we didn't. Becoming a teacher was a natural extension or those who enjoyed and felt like they belonged at school. Those who disliked school came to teaching hoping to impact students more positively, to change the system. Both perspectives considering the idea of school at close range as a collection of individual teachers and students.

Daily teaching tasks also generally operate at this individual-to-group scale. We often only "zoom out" to look at student data at a school, district, or state level. Yet educators tend to develop a keen sense of how systems impact students. We often have nuanced, complex understandings of the challenges that students, families, and communities face. We chose to teach because we either thought that the system worked well, or that we could change it through the way we teach. But if our examinations of patterns of discrepancies in student access and achievement remain too shallow, we're at risk of perpetuating harmful patterns rather than addressing them.

As you seek to heal your relationship with your practice, getting to the heart of the harm is essential. Doing so can be uncomfortable, to say the least. This can be grueling work, as it requires us to scrub the metaphorical wound to eliminate as much debris as possible. That said, doing this wound cleaning at exactly the pace that works for you is also okay. This chapter's information can be intense, even overwhelming, because it explores how we got co-opted, against our best intentions, to enact student-harming values that oppose the values that motivate our work.

Maslow's Hierarchy Literally Missed the Point

We've waited until this chapter to mention Maslow's hierarchy. Weird for a book about self-care, right?

Maslow's hierarchy is everywhere; the kick-off theoretical framework in both teacher prep and professional learning programs, the iconic triangle is often referenced as a fundamental assumption essential to understanding self-care. Of course, we can acknowledge that people must attend to their physical needs to be effective as educators.[35] However, we get into trouble

---

[35] Boogren, T. H. (2018). Take time for you: self-care action plans for educators (using Maslow's hierarchy of needs and positive psychology). Solution Tree Press.

with Maslow's hierarchy when we don't question its core assumptions.

According to Maslow's hierarchy, self-actualization is not only the best that we can do, it's also the ideal we all ought to strive for. Self-actualization is defined as "the realization or fulfillment of one's talents and potentialities, especially considered as a drive or need present in everyone."[36]

The assumption that self-actualization is both the worthiest human goal and a goal that everyone shares has intense implications at societal, organizational, and individual levels. For educators, Maslow's hierarchy may not only harm our sense of worth and agency as educators; it may be the fulcrum on which our desire to contribute to our community is leveraged to trick us into maintaining the poorly-functioning status quo.

Most educators want to contribute to the greater whole, and we attempt to feed this generous impulse in a culture obsessed with individual achievement. Without broader cultural support, we're at risk of overextending ourselves, building resentment, and either leaving the profession we love or harming our relationships with ourselves and our loved ones if we stick around. We're in a real bind accepting self-actualization as a goal, particularly if we agree to be measured based on student achievement on standardized exams. If our self-actualization depends on what other people do within systems we can't totally control, our self-actualization may be a physical impossibility.

The idea of self-actualization can be harmful to an individual. It may also be a foolish ultimate goal in the first place.

What's the Point?

The Maslow's hierarchy that educators know by heart over-simplifies and misrepresents Maslow's work. Despite all of the reasons it shouldn't have been, however, the version of Maslow's hierarchy that we know and are

---

[36] Simpson, J. A., Weiner, E. S. C., & Oxford University Press. (1989). The Oxford English Dictionary. Clarendon Press.

instructed to love (that was designed by a business strategist[37])—is the model photocopied into our welcome-back binders and professional development packets. Though the flaws in the model's creation are well documented and righteous critique continues, Maslow's hierarchy persists.

Having reserved some space and grace for Maslow by acknowledging that we may be working with a bastardization of his work, we also need to put his work into context. The model for which Maslow is so famous fails to acknowledge the Native origins of Maslow's hierarchy, particularly his time spent with the Siksika (Blackfoot) Nation in 1938, how Native worldviews shaped Maslow's thinking (though they weren't properly credited, understood, nor represented in ye olde model), and how current Native scholars are supporting a richer understanding of the Siksika model today. We'll return to these essential ideas later in this chapter.

To remind you why you love teaching and support you to love teaching and yourself in an ongoing fashion, let's name the two most harmful problems built into Maslow's hierarchy. One problem is the way it assumes a linear progression in which one's basic physiological needs must be met in linear time before one can access connection, let alone meaning. Another flaw is that the striped triangle doesn't indicate what we're supposed to use our fancy fulfilled talents and potentialities *for*.

It's Possible to Need—And Access—Multiple Things at Once

Please take care of your basic needs, of course. When and how ever you can. But don't be fooled into thinking that extreme self-care follows a linear progression in which the more basic must be completed before the more complex is begun.

Unfortunately, inevitably, there will be days when you're exhausted, you feel unsafe, and your relationships feel fragile. If it were up to Maslow's hierarchy, you'd be screwed—you'd be denied access to any sense of higher purpose to pull you through. Thankfully, contrary to the way the triangle presents accessing components of self-actualization through time as if we were earning badges, you always have access to your own sense of meaning, which may be exactly what gets you through on some days. If we have to

---

[37] Kaufman, S. (2019) Who created Maslow's iconic pyramid? Scientific American. Retrieved from https://blogs.scientificamerican.com/beautiful-minds/who-created-maslows-iconic-pyramid/

wait to feel loved, connected, financially secure, and well fed before we are allowed to access our sense of purpose? Might as well not get out of bed.

If humans require full bellies before they deserve access to connection and creativity, then Maslow's hierarchy into a gatekeeping device. When we believe that basic need satisfaction must *precede* meaning-making, we allow institutional oppression to masquerade as helpful caring. We see evidence of this all of the time; students in highly impacted schools are forced into achingly boring drill-and-kill math and language arts programs while rich White schools get coding classes and dance programs. The justification? Basic needs before fun. This application is both a perversion of what we know about the learning sciences as well as a perversion of the already-misrepresented ideas in Maslow's hierarchy.

A major component of extreme self-care is the acknowledgment that you are a part of a system and that your participation impacts that system. Suppose you are willing to martyr yourself to a spartan regime in which you'll meet only your basic physiological needs during the school year, and you'll wait for summer to have fun, be curious, nurture relationships, and fully inhabit your humanity. In that case, you're much more likely to do the same to your students. Go ahead and peek back at your values—I would be shocked if all three are about spartan denial, individualistic austerity, or individualistic intellectualism. The structure of this book placed your values exploration in an earlier chapter (Chapter 5) and doesn't acknowledge deep care for your physical self until a later chapter (Chapter 10). This is intentional. Consider the leaders you admire most; if Nelson Mandela, for example, needed three meals a day before he could connect to his purpose, not only would we not know his name, but South Africa's sanctioned apartheid may have continued as it was, unchecked.

Maslow's Hierarchy Forgets That You Are Going to Die

Self-actualization is a limited proposition. I realized this accidentally as a kid.

We lived up a winding mountain road, forty-five minutes from the town where my parents worked. Every day on the drive home, there would be a rich White person, or a whole team of them, riding their bikes up that road. They wore spandex covers over their shoelaces to decrease wind drag. Because the town we commuted to was compulsively obsessed with physical fitness, spandex shoelace covers didn't raise an eyebrow. It was culturally accepted that spending thousands of dollars to lessen a bicycle's weight by an ounce was justifiable. We saw the same people riding the same grueling slope day after day after day. It took tremendous time and effort.

I remember looking at one of the gaunt, straining faces under a helmet and fancy sunglasses and thinking, "What's the point? You're going to die one day. Sure, you're faster and skinnier for now, but who cares? All that work is just going to die with you."

If our selves are our only project, and our selves are perishable, our self-actualization-focused lives are in vain.

Eight-year-old me wasn't on to something new; communities of faith, stoic philosophers, and indigenous communities worldwide had always held similar realizations about the role of self-actualization. They all converge on this idea; self-actualization is limited because our selves are limited.

Granted, it's possible that the athletes in my eight-year-old example were whole humans who, in addition to being committed athletes, were also collaborative community members acting for the common good when they weren't riding up that hill. It's also possible they weren't, and that self-actualization-via-fast-bicycling defined their humanity.

The self-actualization in Maslow's work came from somewhere. In 1938, Maslow spent time with people on the Blackfeet nation, and there happen to be substantial overlaps in key Siksika[38] teachings and what we've come to know as Maslow's hierarchy.[39] Self-actualization is a key feature of the Siksika tribe's model for cultural perpetuity. Self-actualization à la Maslow is an individualistic (read: Western) goal. This is a crying shame because, in addition to appropriating the Siksika's very culture, he got it wrong.

Let's compare Maslow's hierarchy to the Siksika's model. In the Siksika model, humans are not born imperfect, flawed, and expected to meet their basic survival needs before they're allowed to "progress." Rather, humans are born already self-actualized in a community that is already committed to help each individual figure out their unique gifts, and how they can best

---

[38] blackfeetnation.com/our-culture; siksikanation.com
[39] Heavy Head, R., & Blood, N. (2011). Naamitapiikoan: Blackfoot influences on Abraham Maslow's develop-mental and organizational psychology. Alexandria: Microtraining Associates.

contribute those unique gifts for the benefit of the community. If we assume that people are born already whole, sacred, and capable and understand that the role of a community is to nurture their wholeness, sacredness, and capacities, the result is a positive feedback loop.

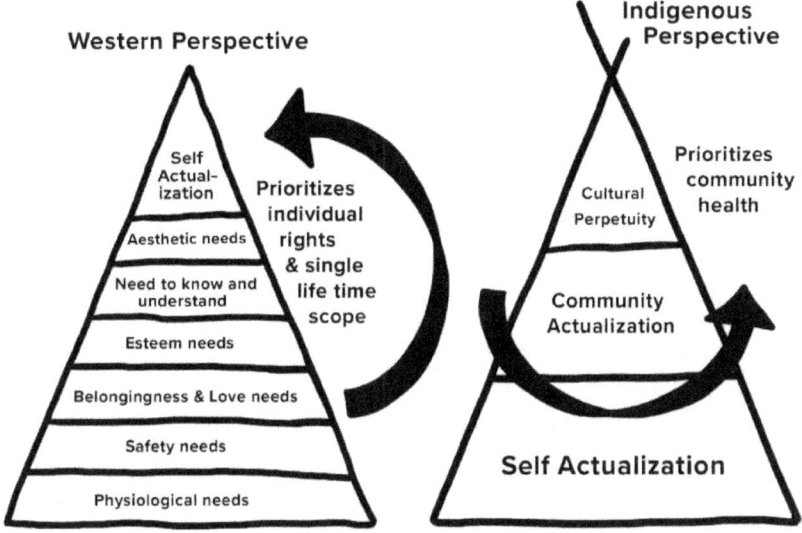

1Graphic image an adaptation of University of Alberta professor Cathy Blackstock's 2014 presentation at the conference of the National Indian Child Welfare Association.

In a 2020 Medium article, Street Data[40] co-author Shane Safir describes the Siksika model this way:

> You'll note that self-actualization is the base of the First Nations tipi... not the peak. After "self" comes community, which is the purpose of becoming an actualized human being—to be of service to our communities as interdependent webs of humanity. And above community...lies cultural perpetuity, or the idea of sustaining cultural values across space, time, and generations.

The Siksika model of the relationship between individual, community, and culture can be hard for a Westerner like me to imagine. My brain was constructed in a culture with Judeo-Christian assumptions that humans are born broken and in need of redemption, and that this world is something to overcome rather than engage with and enrich. That said, it describes the values that connect me to teaching far better than Maslow's hierarchy does. Understanding that there could be such deep, yet subtly enacted, differences in cultural values was an essential step in discovering how my values-motivated approach to my own classroom was co-opted. This realization motivated me to figure out how the values that I didn't agree with were able to sneak into my classroom.

Indigenous Isn't a Synonym

To understand the values that co-opted my practice, I needed to name them and figure out where they came from. While the way Maslow missed the mark with the Siksika folks' ideas is a concrete example of a comparison of values systems, it didn't fully explain the values discrepancies I experienced in my classroom. I started reaching for values systems that aligned with mine. Over and over, these values systems weren't the values enacted by the dominant culture in which I live.

Over and over, I found commonality in cultural values that had a through-line. They were not cultures of colonization. They generally weren't cultures that went to new places and took over by force. My values, and the guiding values of so many of my colleagues, seemed to align best with the values of cultures who had figured out those culturally sustaining practices Maslow missed. Key features defined these distinct values, and it didn't matter if they originated from Bosnia, Belize, Botswana, or Bulgaria. We can refer to these original values, as different from the colonizing values that populate so many communities nowadays, as "Indigenous." Please don't confuse this use of the term "indigenous" with a racial definition. We're not talking about individuals. We mean an ongoing connection to a place in a way that led to a balanced, sustainable community culture over generations (before being interrupted by colonization). To group the dominant cultural values that currently shape our classrooms, we'll refer to that colonizing set of values as "Western."

Western vs. Indigenous Worldviews

To visualize the differences between what I wanted and what I was actually doing, I made a lot of T-charts and tables. Over and over, these tables were organized such that the values I was less excited about aligned with Western values, and those I found motivating aligned with Indigenous values. While my exploration began with common values systems of the Indigenous Americas, as I continue to learn about my own ethnic history in places like pre-colonization Ireland and Hungary, the titles "Indigenous" vs. "Western"[41] seem to hold for many communities that thrived before colonizing contact.

Here's a first pass based on broad ideological categories:

Component	Western	Indigenous
Elemental Human Worth	Flawed from the start, born imperfect; goal of life is to individually strive for perfection and self-actualization	Sacred and whole from the start, born self-actualized; goal of life is to live in contributory and harmonious ways
Information Orientation	Scientific, skeptical, requiring proof	Spiritual, intuitive, believing multiple perspectives
Truth	There is one truth	Many truths can coexist
Identity	Identity is individual and separate from one's connections	Identity comes from connections; everyone and everything is connected
Land	In extractive, impersonal relationship with land	In reciprocal, sacred, balanced relationship with land
Time	Linear—every action leads to a specific, knowable reaction; aging is unfortunate	Cyclical—each day is a new beginning; each developmental stage of life is right and good
Social Status	Determined by success (either material or achievement)	Determined by quality of relationships
Role of Humans	Humans are the most important beings in the world	Humans are not the most important beings in the world
Wealth	Amassing wealth for personal gain is a symbol of power and success	Accumulation is shameful— any additional resources are contributed to those with less

We Need a Different Model

Because schools serve society, applying general ideas from the above table to a classroom context is easy. For my own practice, I got more specific with the ideas in the two columns as I did more of my own work. Thanks to an introduction from the documentary *Precious Knowledge*,[42] I associated that suite of cultural values with a Mayan worldview of In Lak'ech, which translates roughly to, "You are my other self. We are one." Owning an In

---

[41] Joseph, B. (2016). Indigenous peoples' worldviews vs western worldviews. Working Effectively with Indigenous Peoples Blog.

[42] Amor. (2011). Precious Knowledge (Bricca, Ed.). Dos Vatos Productions.

Lak'ech stance means that anything I do to you, I do to myself. Alternately, the Western idea that may matter most for our understanding of this stuff in the context of schools is Cartesian Dualism.

Renée Descartes is the Westerner who named and claimed the separation of mind and body.[43] This separation informed the pre-Maslow hierarchies we're coming to understand so well. If mind and body were separate, mind (closer to heaven, pure [White], logical, male) was better than body (closer to earth, base [dark], emotional, female). Descartes set us up for a whole list of binary values that gives permission to all kinds of -isms still today: racism, sexism, ableism, colorism, and heterosexism, to name a few. If we aren't watching for them, the classroom norms we inherit are as Cartesian as the day is long.

I came to understand the opposing suites of values in my classroom in this way:

Features	Cartesian Dualism at School	Inlak'esh at School
Tagline	"I think, therefore I am."	"I am you and you are me."
Relationship of Parts	Mind-Body Separation	Body-Mind-Spirit Integration
Approach	Competitive	Collaborative
Purpose	Learning is useful for individual gain	Learning is useful for collective benefit
Focus	**Measures** intelligence against a single norm	**Values** multiple ways of knowing

When written out like that, I saw the heart of my demoralization staring me in the face. In the column on the right are the values and beliefs that brought me to the work of teaching and around which I attempted to organize my classroom. The values on the left were the values that permeated the structures, mandates, incentives, and consequences that flooded my practice from every angle, and caused my BD&E.

---

[43] Gutiérrez, J. (2018). Math: It's Not What You "Think". International Society of the Learning Sciences, Inc.[ISLS].

The Medicine Wheel Runs Circles Around Maslow's Hierarchy

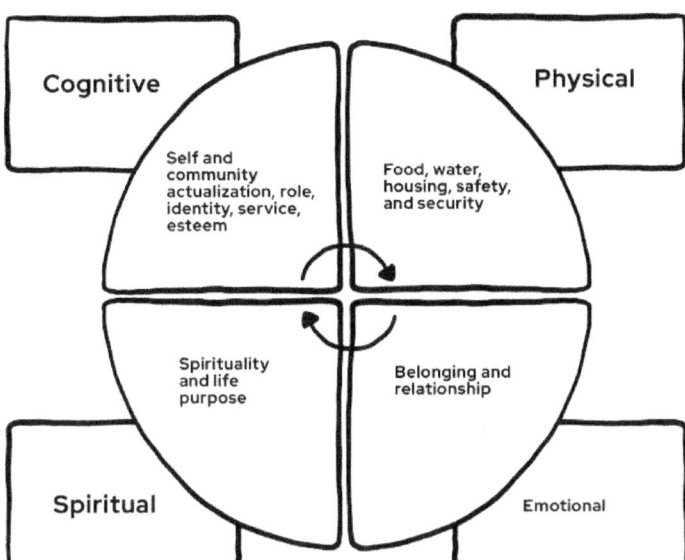

If Maslow's Hierarchy can't articulate what we're trying to do in a classroom, we need something else; teaching is too complex and nuanced to take on without a guiding framework.

Based on the origin story of Maslow's famous triangle, makes sense that a replacement model that felt like a better fit also came from Native American scholarship and work in cultural preservation. As Dr. Cindy Blackstock explains, "The Medicine Wheel holistic model is based on an understanding that all things are affected by the interconnected domains of emotional, physical, spiritual, and cognitive experience."[44]

This model reworks how we think about human needs; in addition to representing cultural practices and perspectives that are tens of thousands of years old, this model also corrects a fundamental weakness in Maslow's hierarchy. The Medicine Wheel model allows for all things to be present at one time; a person can be situated in and integral to their community while simultaneously accessing meaning, relationships, and the material support they need to honor their physiological needs.

---

[44] Blackstock, C. (2011). The emergence of the breath of life theory. Journal of Social Work Values and Ethics, 8(1), 1-16.

Western vs. White Values

More precise than "Western," for those of us living in the USA, "White" may be the most accurate descriptor of our culture's dominant ideology; our culture says the way White people do things is normal, the way White people look is beautiful, and that White people are inherently real, correct, and valuable. This way of thinking undergirds the term "White Supremacy." Far more subtle than marching around carrying a bunch of bigotry and wearing pointy hoods, we don't actually have to be White supremacists to enact White Supremacy. Dang ideological oppression.

This matters to us as educators because Whiteness comes with assumptions and conditions that we may not have been aware of and which likely didn't show up in the list of values that brought us to the classroom.

In U.S. dominant culture a) Whiteness is a thing, and b) it's better than all of the other things. Because White supremacy impacts our culture, including everything from building construction to school day schedules to core standards to our students' daily lived experiences, it is our obligation to understand it. As educators in public schools, it is our double-whammy obligation to understand it, as our classrooms are the intersections where dominant culture messages collide with our students' burgeoning identities.

In our care, our students decide who they are
and whether or not they matter.

If we are accidentally promoting messages about anything other than how capable, perfect (in a sacred sense), and essential they are, we are actively harming our students. Sadly, Whiteness is okay with that. Especially for students of color, but for White students as well.

Whiteness is an invention. I'm White, but only one of my four immigrant grandparents was considered White upon arrival (the English one came aboard already a member of the club, but the Irish, Austrian, and Hungarian ones weren't quite White yet). My ancestors chose to give up much of their culture, language, traditions, and identities in expensive ways. Whiteness must have been worth that cost; the only reason people would pay such a steep price would be for something extremely valuable in return. Then as now, passing as White *is* extremely valuable because White is synonymous with goodness, superiority, and power. And gaining power in a new country where my ancestors didn't know the rules and didn't have things seemed safer than retaining their culturally sustaining ways. I can't judge that choice, but I can mourn it. Simultaneously, I can acknowledge that I benefit from unearned privilege due to their conversion to Whiteness.

That my ancestors weren't considered White—but I am—means that Whiteness is a game with changing rules. The rules for Whiteness are synonymous with the criteria for who gets to attend United States of America party (which began when smallpox completed its first sweep of the continent circa 1941)[45] and, at that party, who has access to the open bar and a karaoke stage, and who has to stay after to clean up. Whiteness is a key to accessing power and privilege. Just because Whiteness is invented doesn't mean it's doesn't have an impact (kinda like the stock market).

The rules of Whiteness have stabilized, and they directly impact your relationship with your classroom. The characteristics of White supremacy culture may, in fact, be the most obvious and direct cause of your BD&E.

Characteristics of White Supremacy in Organizational Culture[46]

The following are excerpts and paraphrased definitions from Kenneth Jones and Tema Okun's "White Supremacy Culture":

- **Perfectionism:** "making a mistake is confused with being a mistake, doing wrong with being wrong"
- **A sense of urgency:** constant pressure (combining insufficient time and vital work) preventing shared decision-making, long-term thinking, or to consider consequences
- **Defensiveness:** people are permitted to respond to new ideas defensively rather than asked to be curious and flexible in thinking
- **Quantity over quality:** little or no value attached to the process; if it can't be measured, it has no value
- **Worship of the written word:** if it's not in a memo, it doesn't exist; if students write an incorrect answer, they know nothing
- **Only one right way:** the belief that when the one right way to do things is introduced the "smart" people join, and resistance is invalid
- **Paternalism:** those with power think they can and should make decisions for and in the interests of those without power

---

[45] Mann, C. C. (2005). 1491: New revelations of the Americas before Columbus. Alfred a Knopf Incorporated.
[46] Jones, K., & Okun, T. (2001). White supremacy culture. Dismantling Racism: A Workbook for Social Change.

- **Either/Or thinking:** things are either good or bad, right or wrong, with us or against us; rejects multiple coexisting truths
- **Power hoarding:** power is seen as limited in quantity, and sharing it is not expected, important, or possible
- **Fear of open conflict:** confusing people who acknowledge difficult issues as being impolite, rude, or out of line
- **Individualism:** people in the organization believe they are responsible for solving problems alone and seek competitive praise and recognition rather than teamwork
- **I'm the only one:** connected to individualism, the belief that if something is going to get done right, 'I' have to do it without delegating or sharing
- **Progress is bigger/more:** success is defined by changes in the metrics that have been chosen, with an emphasis on increasing "progress" without acknowledging the potential cost
- **Objectivity:** the belief that it is possible to think and act neutrally and that emotions are inherently destructive, irrational, and should not play a role in decision-making or group process
- **Right to comfort:** those in power are entitled to emotional and psychological comfort at any cost

Classroom Culture = White Supremacy Culture

Values are enacted through actions. To track down how unwelcome values had supplanted my own values and commandeered my teaching practice, I had to learn a little more about how, exactly. Understanding "White Supremacy Culture" helped bridge this gap for me. When I first encountered this definition of White supremacy culture, I felt like the curtain had been drawn back to reveal the meta-cultural Oz who had secretly been pulling the levers of my practice the whole time. We'll explore the list of these cultural characteristics, then go item by item to see how each can look in schools and classrooms.

The characteristics that showed up in my daily experiences in schools most reliably were: a sense of urgency, defensiveness, quantity over quality, worship of the written word, paternalism, power hoarding, fear of open conflict, and a right to comfort.

Urgency as a value, however manufactured, showed up from every direction. District initiatives were to be implemented yesterday. Parent concern was allowed to interrupt instruction. It didn't seem to matter what the issue was— everything was just... urgent. This created what I experienced as a perpetual heightening of an already high-stress expectation of building and facilitating high-quality instruction for a beautiful pile of perpetually dynamic humans every day. When I inquired earnestly about the urgency of triaging my workflow, I was often greeted with defensiveness.

Defensiveness alone would have been okay if there was a culture established that supported working through it or arguing to get closer to the truth. Because White supremacy culture also believes that there is only one correct answer, any question I asked was interpreted as an attack, an attempt to argue to be right. Because there was also fear of open conflict combined with entrenched power hoarding, I often felt shut out, gossiped about, or like I wasn't a part of the "in" team. For someone who values collaboration, I experienced these rifts as equal parts painful and baffling.

Paternalism, worship of the written word, and a right to comfort governed how I was supposed to interact with my colleagues and how we approached our students' families. Required benchmarks and end-of-level exams, informed by standardized exams' role in upholding White supremacy,[47] communicate that the exam authors know best about what is worth knowing. Paternalistic mandates from state, district, and school-level administrators were, almost invariably, presented via thick binders and fill-in-the-blank forms. This worship of the written word was evidence of the organization valuing product over process—also in stark contrast with my own values. Finally, the right to comfort, like defensiveness, allowed those who acted the most offended or fragile to get their way. If someone couldn't self-regulate, then in the name of conflict management, teams bent to the will of the most reactive member, leading to decisions that had little do with student outcomes. I watched teams become more likely to tantrum over time because team members had seen that tantruming was an effective way to dodge scrutiny and get their way.

My colleagues and school structures didn't have to do all of the heavy

---

[47] Zenderland, L. (2001). Measuring minds: Henry Herbert Goddard and the origins of American intelligence testing. Cambridge University Press.

lifting; I took up plenty of White supremacy characteristics internally. Perfectionism gripped me, kept me at school until 6 p.m. only to bring home more grading and planning. I didn't specifically think I wanted to be perfect, it just felt like I could work forever and not be the teacher that I was expected to be. Perfectionism motivated me to keep trying anyway, even though I understood that it was an impossible set-up.

In addition to my collegial isolation, I brought my own "I'm the only one" hero story to my practice. I wanted to be "different," I wanted to "matter." These desires are okay if they aren't held in a competitive stance. Because schools are currently competitive places, it's impossible to not be pushed into comparison. I, along with many of my colleagues, wanted to matter *more*.

Here are more examples:

Characteristic	Observable Examples	Educator Experiences
Perfectionism	Districts, schools, and administrators don't feel safe publicly sharing real challenges	Procrastination Hyper-focus on details that don't improve instruction Student deficit orientation
A Sense of Urgency	Rapid shifts in district-wide programming Grade-level proficiency goals regardless of students' incoming skills	A perpetual sense of rushing to "cover the curriculum"
Defensive-ness	Restrictive data-sharing agreements Limited community or public-private partnerships	Reluctance to be observed Responding intensely/emotionally to suggestions and critiques
Quantity Over Quality	A push to "cover" curriculum Over-enrolling courses (particularly "remedial" courses)	Facilitating a constant stream of teacher-built activities without supported time for students to struggle and generate
Worship of the Written Word	Preference for classrooms in which students are seated and writing (vs. speaking or moving)	Feeling pressure to grade everything that students produce Reliance on written policies over relational culture building to "manage" student behavior
Only One Right Way	Preference for standardized assessments designed to evaluate a narrow band of culturally contextual content	Fixation on controlling students' physical and verbal behaviors unrealed to learning

Characteristic	Observable Examples	Educator Experiences
Paternalism	The state, district, or administrator knows better than the educator	The teacher knows better than the students and their families
Either/Or Thinking	Tracking students Denying low-scoring students "enrichment" programming	Labeling students (good/bad, quick/slow, supported/needy)
Power Hoarding	Educators with more time and experience deliberately assigning heavier, more challenging loads to early-career educators	Punitive discipline[48] Unclear expectations for assignment/evaluation criteria
Fear of Open Conflict	"School Resource "Officers" (threat of violence as pre-emptive conflict squashing)	Dismissing earnest student grievances, or even inquiries, about challenging topics
Individualism	Schools within a district competing with each other (re: scores, resources, etc)	Educators transferring students that challenge them into other colleagues' classrooms
I'm the Only One	Administrators unilaterally making school goals like becoming a 90/90/90 school[49]	Teachers (without clinical training) encouraging students to confide personal traumas in order to feel important
Progress = Bigger/More	Over-stuffed classrooms Sweeping reform packages Over-full content standards	"Covering" the curriculum A teacher who parks in one position for years without seeking learning or growth, who feels superior to those who change positions
Objectivity	State standards written by educators and content experts without community or stake-holder input	Educators' tendencies to interpret student behavior as if their interpretation is the objective truth about a student's experience
Right to Comfort	Districts, schools, and admin-istrators rarely seeking authentic input from teachers or stakeholders	Educators (sans clinical training) diagnosing and dismissing students they have been unable to effectively support

---

[48] Dillard, C. (2020, Fall). The weaponization of whiteness in schools. Teaching for Justice, 65. Retrieved from https://www.learningforjustice.org/magazine/fall-2020/the-weapon-ization-of-whiteness-in-schools

[49] Lemar, A. S. (2019). Building bridges and breaking down walls: taking integration seriously in CED practice. Journal of Affordable Housing & Community Development, 28(2). 207-211.

Every System Is Perfectly Designed to Get the Results It Gets

I wish that your BD&E was an incidental byproduct of a system that suffers from benign neglect. If it were just you, out of millions of teachers, or even just a couple hundred thousand, it would be more possible to blame BD&E on individual educators. As you know, it's not just an educator here or there who is suffering. Educators are suffering. As are students. With this background in mind, it's easier to be open to the possibility that what is happening is not, in fact, accidental.

The cruel truth is that our public school system works the way it does on purpose. While benign neglect would be a more comfortable answer, we're in the business of wound-cleaning, and so we are obligated to be straightforward and incisive in this claim; the United States of America's public education system was originally built, and continues to function, more as a tool for oppression than liberation. Intentionally.

It is intentional that socioeconomic status has been—and remains— the number one predictor of student academic success.[50] It's intentional that 80% of our nation's families who enroll their children in private schools are what the U.S. Department of Education calls "nonpoor." It's intentional that teacher pay is nearly 20% lower than salaries of careers that require similar entry-level training (controlled for "summers off").[51]

The socioeconomic structure of our nation relies on disproportionate access to power and opportunity. Public, private, and charter schools all play roles in ensuring that some people have access and some people don't. We educators get into trouble when we pretend that these patterns are accidental. This willful non-acknowledgment sets us up for BD&E; when we severely underestimate the forces motivating an extremely stable-but-harmful system, our personal instability increases as we find ourselves less able to impact the system in meaningful ways.

To survive the stacked deck and thrive, in the classroom and beyond, we have to rigorously honest about the factors motivating a system that's so likely to harm its participants (both educators and students alike). Having

---

[50] American Psychological Association. (2017). Education and socioeconomic status factsheet. Retrieved August, 2021, from https://www.apa.org/pi/ses/resources/publications/ factsheet-education.pdf

[51] Allegretto, S., & Mishel, L. (2018). The teacher pay penalty has hit a new high: Trends in the teacher wage and compensation gaps through 2017. Economic Policy Institute.

named them, we then get to choose to act in the service of our own values rather than those imposed on us. This is different than the "find your why" often suggested to struggling educators. Identifying your "why" alone won't heal you. Healing demands more. You not only have to "find your why," you have to enact your "why" in your classroom and your life. Daily. You have to be able to know when you are actively serving your values instead of values imposed upon you.

Shifting to prioritize your values over the system's doesn't just happen. You need to plan for it.

Too Long; Didn't Read
Chapter 6:
Maslow's Hierarchy Missed the Point

Ideas

- Maslow's hierarchy claims that we need to have our material needs met before our social and spiritual needs can be met and before we can be self-actualized.
- Indigenous models say we are born self-actualized and that connection to community and meaning is as essential as meeting physical needs.
- Western values often align with demoralizing practices. Indigenous values often align with the values that brought educators into the work in the first place.
- Characteristics of White Supremacy Culture often define the values that we least connect with as educators (find list on p. 91).
- What we say school is for and what school is actually for are different, and this difference causes dissonance for educators.

Strategies

- Examine the Characteristics of White Supremacy Culture and:
  - explore how they might be impacting your instructional context
  - compare them to the values you'd like to guide your own practice
  - use this comparison to find opportunities to set internal and external boundaries to protect your service to your own values

Section
2

How and When

Chapter 7

Your Calendar Is Your Life

In which we map out the year, ensuring that our personal lives are protected and that our professional timelines are set up with plenty of room for our students to be students and our values to show up in our work.

"The times are urgent. We must slow down."
— Bàyò Akómoláfé —

"Happiness is when what you think, what you say, and what you do are all in harmony."
— Mahatma Gandhi —

Reflexive Backward Planning

As educators, we know how important it is to identify how we'll know they know; in other words, if our students are successful at mastery, how would they show us that? For many of us, the first step in building a learning progression to support the answer to that question was "backward planning," a central tenet of Wiggins' and McTighe's seminal Understanding By Design.[52] If we start by designing the assessment that answers, "How will we know they know?" and then ask, "How will we build an instructional sequence to ensure that students can demonstrate mastery?" we're more likely to be successful than if we string a bunch of activities together and cross our fingers before handing out last year's multiple-choice exam.

---

[52] Wiggins, G. P., Wiggins, G., & McTighe, J. (2005). Understanding by design. ASCD.

To be successful in enacting empowered self-care, we need to think about our own intended outcomes in the same way. In order for us to pull together our self-knowledge, self-care, values, and commitments (both inside and outside of the classroom), we need to know what we're shooting for. While you can do the following activities at any time, do honor the your planning by creating quiet, spacious time to focus deeply. For many of us, the best time of year for "planning to stay" might be early August-ish.

Reflection vs. Reflexivity

Often, we describe meta-level work like this as "reflection." Planning to stay is actually a reflexive task.

Excellent teachers are reflective practitioners. Reflection is an in-depth consideration of events or situations: the people involved, what they experienced, and how they felt about it. This involves reviewing or reliving an experience to bring it into focus and replaying it from different points of view. Most educators get practice with reflecting on lessons and interactions in both our teacher prep programs and in collegial interactions, even if it's just debriefing an experience informally over lunch. Reflection focuses on external circumstances, the who-did-what-and-why. Reflective conclusions can inform our external choices in instruction; reflection may change how we order a lesson, build a worksheet, or greet a student.

While reflection is essential for a vital teaching practice, it's only half the battle. For those of us facing burnout, demoralization, and exploitation (BD&E), it's our internal experience that deserves some attention.

Reflexive practitioners attend to their internal experience and how their internal experience impacts others.

To be reflexive is to observe our internal worlds the same way reflection supports our external worlds. Reflexivity helps us become aware of the role our needs and desires play in motivating our choices. Reflexivity helps us see how our behavior is complicit in forming organizational practices which, for example, marginalize groups or exclude individuals.

Doing the deep, gruelingly honest self-examination required in order to address your BD&E will benefit the way you feel in and out of the classroom. More importantly, it will benefit the people in your classroom and in your world who feel better and better when spending time with you.

What Will Alignment Look Like for You?

A values-centered practice is one in which a practitioner can clearly identify how their guiding values motivate, impact, and support their instructional decisions. Practicing in congruence with your values is your surest way to escape demoralization. Depending upon your interpretation of your values, sticking with them can also help you to combat burnout and exploitation.

You've identified your own values. I've shared some examples of how I practiced out of alignment. In the following activity, you'll spend some time crafting concrete connections between your values and how you enact them in the classroom and your life. As you build your vision for yourself in your reflexive examination, it helps to consider what you'll want to know, feel, and be able to do. This will apply to four areas of your experience: your internal and external experiences in your classroom and your internal and external experiences in your personal life.

What you'd like to "know" are the ideas, stances, theoretical frameworks, or approaches that explain, specifically, how your values connect to your teaching practice. They are also the statements that serve as our "north stars." They are perfect ideas that keep us focused when we are not perfect. They are an articulation of the practitioner we hope to be. You'll get a chance to think about this from four perspectives:
- internal work you will do to align your teaching practice
- external changes you will enact to change your practice
- internal work you will do to honor yourself in your personal life
- external changes you will enact to honor yourself in your personal life

Once you've named what you'd like to know in these four realms (internal and external, classroom and life), you'll explore how you'd like to feel. It's critical to consider how you'll feel in your planning process for two reasons: to protect your professional integrity and to promote your personal wellbeing. By articulating how you hope to feel, you're acknowledging that you're a person in the room, that you do, indeed, have feelings, and that these feelings impact both you and your students.

Once you've acknowledged that your feelings impact your professionalism, you can be more aware of your feelings as indicators, as invitations to explore what changes you want to make. If you aren't feeling how you had hoped to, it's a chance to wonder if you're being infringed upon by perfectionism, say, or a paternalistic mandate that you've internalized. Being able to understand and be in conversation with your feelings supports you to be responsive instead of reactive.

Finally, once you've identified what you hope to know and feel, you're ready to think about what you will do, specifically, based on what you know and how you wish to feel. This seems simple, but the hinge between what we know and feel and what we do is where it's easiest to get out of alignment. For example, one educator I coached valued empowering her students to be advocates and activists within their community. Day after day, however, her instruction consisted of direct instruction and a couple of well-crafted discussion prompts by which students would confirm the information she had shared. She was puzzled that she wasn't feeling inspired and excited by her practice when she was so committed to her value of empowering students. When she was able to explain what she would look for if she were watching her class like a movie with the sound off, what student actions would tip her off that her students were being empowered as advocates and activists, she was able to shift her instruction to a more student-centered frame. Her enthusiasm peaked when she was able to serve as a "guide on the side" instead of a "sage on stage," when she was able to act in alignment with her values by supporting students to ask and strive to answer their own questions.

When you think about what you'll do, you're also asking, "How will my students' and my loved ones' experiences of me change if I'm enacting my values?" Building actions in which your values are apparent, evident, embodied, and unmistakable in your teaching practice is the way you'll change your internal experience and, consequently, how others experience you.

> Your increased spaciousness and gentle self-curiosity
> will immediately impact how you relate to your students.

The following table contains some examples of possible backward-planning-inspired "planning to stay" metrics. If any of the examples align with your values, feel free to use them. If not, write ones that work best for you, your values, and your life.

EXAMPLE	
Guiding Values	1. Relationships 2. Autonomy 3. Creativity
Realm	**If you are successful at "planning to stay," what will you know, feel, and be able to do?**
Classroom: My INTERNAL experience	Know: Connecting with students as people is more important than reactive rule enforcement. Feel: Calm, present Be able to do: Identify when I feel stressed and calm myself before I react to a student in a way that will harm their trust in me.
Classroom: My EXTERNAL experience	Know: I trust students to co-manage our classroom environment. Feel: Confident that students can access the resources they need to successfully meet high expectations. Be able to do: Build a classroom that empowers students to get materials, catch up on missing work, clean up, and know what our plans without interrupting instruction.
Personal life: My INTERNAL experience	Know: When I am a whole person outside of the classroom I'm a kinder person inside the classroom. Feel: Confident that I am capable, and I will still create meaningful learning episodes even if I'm not consumed by teaching in all of my spare time. Be able to do: Recognize when I'm obsessing about work during family meals and refocus on being present and pleasant with my loved ones.
Personal life: My EXTERNAL experience	Know: I am a better spouse when I I can manage my stress enough to participate in our daily household chores. Feel: Contributory to our home life during the school year, not just summers. Be able to do: Exercise at least 3x/week to manage stress, and tidy the kitchen nightly during the school year to honor my partner's preferences.

ACTIVITY: How Will You Know Your Planning Is Working?

Guiding Values	1. 2. 3.
Realm	**If you are successful at "planning to stay," what will you know, feel, and be able to do?**
Classroom: My INTERNAL experience	Know: Feel: Be able to do:
Classroom: My EXTERNAL experience	Know: Feel: Be able to do:
Personal life: My INTERNAL experience	Know: Feel: Be able to do:
Personal life: My EXTERNAL experience	Know: Feel: Be able to do:

Calendar Like You Mean It!

For the following activity, you'll need all of the calendars that impact your life (district academic calendars, curriculum maps, etc.). You'll also need the calendars of important people in your life (or, if not their whole calendar, dates of events that matter to them). We'll build your calendar to support your values-connected practice by using it to represent all parts of you and your practice. If, at any point, there is some part of your life that is important to you that isn't listed here, please add it, and get it on your calendar!

ACTIVITY: Calendaring Your Year

It's time to get to planning! Use the following checklist to support you in planning to stay:

Academic Calendar Dates

- ☐ First contract day
- ☐ Last contract day
- ☐ First day of classes
- ☐ End of term
- ☐ Start of term
- ☐ Holidays

Educator Obligations

- ☐ Back-to-School Night (or similar)
- ☐ Family-Educator conferences (or similar)
- ☐ Dates and exact times grades are due for each term
- ☐ Faculty meetings
- ☐ Grade-level, subject, and other collaboration meetings
- ☐ Testing windows—benchmarks
- ☐ Testing windows—end-of-levels
- ☐ Committee meetings
- ☐ Coaching and after-school program
- ☐ Performances, banquets, and other school-related events
- ☐ Administrator observations
- ☐ Administrator evaluations
- ☐ Additional meetings re: next year's course assignments

Even if you don't know the exact dates, block off time for these things. This will allow you to better anticipate. You can always move time blocks.

Personalize Your Checklist

In addition to the checklist above, which lists predictable components of a teacher's tasks and responsibilities, you'll want to calendar components of your own life with just as much commitment to protect time for them. The following lists include additional events that you may want to consider, and ways to think about the order and organization of your life and classroom. If something is missing from this list, add it.

You know your life best.

Personal Have To

- ☐ **Routine health appointments** (doctor(s), dentist, etc.)
  Schedule appointments now so that your time is protected, and you don't suddenly go three years without getting your teeth cleaned. It's tempting to save this for summer. Please don't.
- ☐ **Financial and legal deadlines** (when rent is due, court dates, etc.)
- ☐ **Routine home/auto maintenance** (oil/filter changes, etc.)

Personal Want To

- ☐ **Your birthday**
  It doesn't matter how you feel about it; no one's forcing you to take the day off. You matter, even if the anniversary of your birth occurs during the school year. Get it on the calendar because this calendar is your life, and you can acknowledge your adventure's anniversary.
- ☐ **Family and friends' birthdays**
- ☐ **Events, festivals, and seasonal or time-sensitive activities**
  (ex: If you hate hot weather but love being outside in the autumn, you might mark which weekends are likely to be within temps ideal for a barbeque or camping trip during term 1).

Consider doing this "Personal Want To" step at least twice per school year, once before the school year starts and once after the first term ends (and, perhaps, at the close of every term), with the people in your life who you'd like to plan with, particularly if they are not educators.

Inspiring Instruction

☐ **Final Project Deadlines**

This is not the same as the end of the term, nor the day that grades are due. Consider making final projects, or anything summative that requires time to grade, due well before your grades are due, even if that means it's due a week or two before the actual end of the term.

☐ **Grading**

When will you grade the above-mentioned final projects? Is this timeline likely to change? Yes. Are you more likely to stay sane if you represent the actual time it's going to take on your calendar so that you don't bail on important parts of your life three or four times a year because grades are predictably due? Also yes. By blocking off the time, you can move the time blocks without forgetting that this task will require time.

☐ **High-Stress Windows**

Note times that are more intense for you, personally, as a date range where you may need to lighten up in other areas. You may avoid planning energy-intensive self-care trips during those times, or plan instructional sequences that require less energy for you to facilitate.

☐ **Low-Morale Windows**

Note when you tend to struggle with morale (February and March are well-documented as challenging months for educators, but you may have additional times of year that are tough for you). When considering these windows, plan how you'll infuse them with authentic positivity, hope, and anything that boosts your mood.

For example, someone who manages seasonal affective disorder may plan easier lessons during December's shortest days, while someone mourning the anniversary of a loved ones' passing in October may want to plan their favorite unit during that time to focus on something positive and actionable.

Routine Self Care

☐ **Calendar one high-value self-care activity per week.**
Find your list of things you like to do and the self-care categories they support. High value activities satisfy three or more self-care categories.

☐ **Calendar one "look forward to" event each month.**
If there are times without events, birthdays, etc., plan something specific that you'll look forward to, even if it's a movie with friends or cooking something new that you've wanted to try.

☐ **Protect an hour for yourself.**
Pick one hour per weekday when you will, without question, not be working; you may not include your commute, nor when you're trying to sleep.

☐ **Protect a day for yourself.**
Pick one weekend day out of every weekend when you will, without question, not be working. Consider communicating this day to the people in your life with whom you want to stay connected. Letting them know that you're most likely able to keep plans the night before this day and this day itself will help them to honor your boundaries while increasing the likelihood that you'll be able to hang out.

☐ **Let your email work for you.**
Change your email signature and disclosure document language to communicate any boundary that, if you were clear about, would help both protect your time and support positive communication expectations for colleagues, students, and families. Framing things as positives, like Dr. Santoro's "I check email once per day, and will respond within 48 working hours" may lead to more positive interactions for you over time compared to something like "My personal time is my personal time, your emergency isn't my emergency, I'll get to your email when I can."

Too Long; Didn't Read
Chapter 7:
Your Calendar Is Your Life

Ideas

- Your internal and external experiences impact you and your students.
- Taking responsibility for your own self-regulation is the best thing you can do to improve your students' experience in your classroom.
- You can use your time to support the best version of yourself in and out of the classroom.
- External deadlines don't need to dictate your timeline. As long as you can honor your obligations, you get to use your planning in a way that works best for you, regardless of external deadlines.

Strategies

- Set specific goals for how you'd like to feel and behave, both inside and outside of the classroom to enact your values (activity pp. 105-106).
- Intentionally calendar with your values in mind, both inside of the classroom and out (list of things to keep in mind pp. 107-110).

Chapter 8

Rehumanize Your Lesson Plans

In which we infuse your instruction with self-care principles for you and your students toward an authentic, revitalizing classroom community.

"What the educator does in teaching is to make it possible for the students to become themselves."
— Paolo Freire —

A Humanized Example

Before we explore rehumanizing instruction in an in-classroom way, we'll begin by comparing our human students to a non-human species. We can think of our relationships with students as analogous to human's relationship with horses. Please note: our work involves humans, who are neither animals nor property, who have intrinsic and equal value no matter their age, race, gender, class, ability, or creed (Oh, hey, Descartes! We see you assuming that non-human species are inferior).

Here, I mean to compare students to horses due to the parallels of tricksy, high-pressure, power-impacted collaborations. That is all.

When I was a kid, I spent time with horses. There was no way "having" a horse would happen financially, so from the age of nine, I started shoveling poop to be around the mesmerizing creatures. I suspect the same thing that draws me to teaching is what drew me to working with horses; being in merged teamwork, in sync, working together for a shared goal (even if the goal is as arbitrary as running around a barrel), that's my happy place.

My job was to finish "green broke" horses so that they could perform in shows. These young horses had already been saddled and had learned to take a bridle (a metal bar) in their mouths to serve as a steering wheel. Holding a metal bar in one's mouth, wearing a saddle made of skin from another prey animal—these are not natural experiences for a young horse. While it's obviously untenable to think about these actions in parallel with students, it's not as far off as we'd hope. Don't we inflict similar physical discomfort when we ask energetic muscles and growing bodies to stay mushed between chairs and desks all day? Don't we ask students to be in terrifying proximity to ideas and even people (think School Resource Officers), that would be dangerous to encounter in other settings?

It requires skill to train horses to accept this bridle-and-saddle arrangement. Because not everyone has skill, some trainers use mean tricks to make up for their lack. Even if I didn't know the approach the trainer used, it was often easy to guess by the reactions in the horses themselves when they got to me after being saddled and bridled. They split into two categories—horses who were scared, and horses who were curious.

There are parallels in the relationships between humans and horses and teachers and students. These parallels include an artificial hierarchical power structure which, because it's artificial, is always at risk of being challenged.

In human-horse interactions, human responses to power-related challenges are either motivated by brutality or patience, power or love. The horses who had been "saddle-broke" arrived scared. Their early trainers believed they had to be *broken*. They had been whipped into submission, sometimes literally. Those who arrived curious, however, had been invited into collaboration in ways that honored their worth and experience of wonder. The curious horses hadn't been forced into submission—rather, they'd been invited into a reciprocal relationship in which they would be taken care of by the powerful humans who were also asking them to do weird stuff.

We, as educators, ask kids to do weird stuff all of the time. During the time of their development when their bodies are most wiggly, we ask them to sit and stay. When they are biologically craving social interactions, we ask them to face forward silently (in traditional classrooms, at least). As growing humans, they are full of thoughts connected to their rich experiences and feelings connected to those thoughts, and we ask them to put that stuff aside and focus on topics selected for them by State Boards of Education.

We can motivate students to participate in unnatural behaviors from one of two sides of human capacity: brutality or patience, power or love.

Winning Over Time Beats Winning In The Moment

When I was a child, my grandmother took me to see the Lipizzaners. To my grandmother, these famous stallions symbolized her pre-Holocaust life in Vienna. To me, they embodied the quiet alignment I'm so drawn to in both inter- and intra-human collaborations. The tickets for the show were expensive. I remember being aware of that expense through every second of the performance and forcing myself to soak up and enjoy every detail instead of simply being overwhelmed by guilt (good job, Inner Child!).

At the end of the show, the trainer stood in the dirt with his back to the audience. Three horses, free of saddles and bridles, lined up shoulder-to-shoulder facing him (and us). Without touching the horses and without raising his voice, using only gestures to cue them, he asked the three horses to turn, trot, weave around each other, and rear up on their back legs. They trusted him; there was no hesitation between him asking and them executing. Until there was.

At the close of the act, the trainer asked the horses to bow. It was an uncomfortable, vulnerable position; they stretched a front hoof forward and pointed their noses at that downward foot, briefly lifting their other front leg to "wave." The youngest and feistiest horse wouldn't do it.

The trainer ignored the audience; not through effort, he just didn't offer us any awareness. He took a slow, visible deep breath. He asked again. The horse refused (meanwhile, the other two held the bow the whole time—whoa). The trainer shook out his shoulders, softly walked up to the non-bowing horse, used a more exaggerated hand motion, and asked again. The horse threw his head back and corkscrew-reared away in a decidedly non-choreographed way. After several seconds of sprinting in circles, the not-gonna-do-it horse stopped off-center and behind the two bowing horses. The audience members, hundreds of us, collectively held our breath.

The trainer laughed. Not to the audience. Not at the rebelling horse. He laughed *with* the rebelling horse. It wasn't a laugh of meanness. It was gentle and loving. He praised and released the other two horses from their earnestly held shapes and, still laughing, turned to the audience and shrugged. The audience, relieved, laughed and shrugged with him, loving that little horse and the safety the trainer gave him to not be feeling the bow trick.

Let's imagine how that could have gone. What if the trainer was caught up in the self-righteous, I'm-here-to-help-you-damnit-how-you-perform-is-who-I-am state of stress that so many of us educators find ourselves in? What if, running through his head, were thoughts like, "These people paid good money to see you do this bow thing, so you're going to do a bow thing!" He could have stomped. He could have made a big show of how disappointed he was, how this kind of thing never happens, how dismayed he was that one of his horses dared to be so insubordinate. He could have let us all know how much better he is than that horse's refusal, how bad that horse is for not doing what he was told. He could have proven how much he cared about our opinions by punishing that horse. And, in so doing, he could have damaged his relationship with that horse forever.

But he didn't. He took deep breaths. He shook out his shoulders. He tried a few different things. He let himself be defined by his approach, and he loosened his grip on the outcome. He was clear that the relationship was his priority, a guiding value. He courageously prioritized connection and compassion over his audience-aware ego. He calmly approached the challenge with creativity, and he was confident enough in himself and in the horse's development over time that that solitary moment didn't define him.

I learned more about classroom management from that interaction than from all of the books I've read and trainings I've attended, combined. The trainer showed me how foolish it is to think we can control the beings in our care. The best we can do is understand who they truly are, what motivates them, and attempt to meaningfully connect to those motivations. When it doesn't work, we don't need to take it personally. Their failure to do the thing we wanted is not our failure; we only fail when we don't self-regulate, when we harm them when we act out of poorly mediated stress.

Responding effortlessly requires a lot of work.

The work of being so deeply present feels different than the productivity-obsessed, stress-fueled over-work we're trying to unlearn in this book (and in our lives). Prioritizing productive relationships with students means naming, connecting with, and supporting your own needs as a human, and as separate from your students' needs and choices. It means letting them be who they are, doing our best to meet them where they are, and fortifying ourselves enough that, when they don't behave the way we'd hoped, we can shrug, chuckle good-naturedly, love them as inherently valuable and autonomous, and try again (with our values-aligned relationships intact).

Of course, we want both; we wish that we could have both excellent relationships with students and that students will consistently demonstrate learning progress. If we prioritize outcomes, it only takes one bummer outcome, one time we react from our disappointed striving instead of our values, to eliminate all future chances of growth with a student. If we prioritize relationships, then we have some hope of recovering after the inevitable times when students don't feel like prioritizing showing us what they are learning.

Use Your Instruction to Remoralize Your Practice

Burnout, demoralization, and exploitation depend on us letting go of some core part of our humanity to keep doing the job. This self-abandonment doesn't just impact us as individuals. The painful part of this process is that BD&E can dehumanize our relationships with our students, the very humans we started out so committed to helping.

The fastest route to BD&E is to accept an adversarial stance regarding your students. If you start noticing yourself giving mean-spirited nicknames to students (or groups, or types of students), if you start making defensive decisions like preventing cheating rather than making an assessment so authentic that it happens to be impossible to cheat, if students feel like the enemy—then you know you're in a classroom that's being dehumanized.

Anyone who has spent 20 seconds in a classroom knows that no matter how beautiful your lesson plans are nor how impeccably you've calendared your year, the real-live humans in the room outnumber you, and their unpredictable states and experiences will impact your instruction. This reality can be discouraging, even scary. But it doesn't have to be—particularly if we have our eight Cs (creativity, courage, curiosity, a sense of connection, compassion, clarity, calm, and confidence) around.

We'll spend this chapter exploring the nuts-and-bolts decisions you can make to rehumanize your instruction on a curriculum-map, lesson-plan, and moment-to-moment scales. But first, a definition for the process:

> Unlike "equity," which can seem to represent a destination, "rehumanizing" is a verb; it reflects an ongoing process and requires constant vigilance to maintain and to evolve with contexts.
>
> ...Rehumanizing is an ongoing performance and requires evidence

from those for whom we seek to rehumanize our practices that, in fact, the practices are felt in that way... we do not need to invent something new; we simply need to return to full presence that which tends to get erased through the process of schooling.[53]

Dehumanized classrooms are both a cause and effect of structural opp-ression. In rehumanized classrooms, educators intentionally use positional power to encourage rather than to dominate. Rehumanized classrooms allow students and teachers to be whole people enjoying and believing in each other and who are work collaboratively for enduring learning.

Self-Management is Deep Classroom Management

There are lots of books on classroom management. You can find a book to support any approach. What many of these books leave out, however, is that it doesn't matter what method you use because "every tool is a weapon, if you hold it right."[54] If you are stressed out, resentful, and taking things personally, you can use your gorgeously co-created classroom norms to punish the students who bug you—in ways that are likely perpetuating bias and harming those students' learner identities in long-lasting ways. If you are centered in yourself and your values, if you are caring for yourself and showing up as the adult in the room, you can take any school-mandated token economy disguised as the newest "positive behavior intervention system" and turn bribery into reciprocal caring, feedback, and buy-in.

Who and how you are in your classroom are the most important ingredients to your management success.

It's important to acknowledge here that humans are, in fact, humans. We respond to incentives and disincentives. Because human children are, in fact, human children, it is a biological mandate that they push our boundaries and, often, our buttons. Our work is to:

- accept that students pushing boundaries (and buttons) is inevitable
- not take it personally when students push boundaries
- care for ourselves sufficiently as the adult in the room to ensure that we
- have the internal resources necessary to respond according to our values (instead of react according to our egos) when our buttons are pushed

[53] Goffney, I., Gutiérrez, R., & Boston, M. (2018). Rehumanizing mathematics for Black, Indigenous, and Latinx students. National Council of Teachers of Mathematics.
[54] DiFranco, A. (1993). My IQ [Song]. On Puddle dive. Righteous Babe Records.

- greet our students with perpetual opportunities to become the best version of themselves —as they learn to define that for themselves, and no matter how many times they chose differently before

If you aren't getting the behavior you want from students, it's not personal; it's an invitation to examine your incentive structure and to adjust incentives to support the behavior you're hoping for.

That secret contract that you, as a helper, tricked them into signing without their knowledge or consent? It usually goes something like, "Their only job in society is to be students right now; they need to take this as seriously as I am," or, "Their families don't know how school works in the U.S.; they're lucky to have my support at all," or, "I care about them, so they should care about me." All of these examples are non-consensual and non-explicit. If you're resenting students for their failure to honor an invisible contract, you're setting everybody up for failure.

Your students are forced to be in your room. You can play the phony semantics game by telling them that "you always have a choice," but that's a lie, too, and kids are good at spotting dishonesty. How can you avoid BD&E? By acknowledging that your students have to be with you, that they owe you nothing, and that their response to your incentive system is meaningful data that you'd benefit from noting without taking personally.

In a rehumanized classroom, when students inevitably do things differently than you hoped or expected, their reactions become data instead of personal attacks. You get to wonder, "What didn't work, and what might?". This is more fun, less damaging, and more survivable than, "What is wrong with them?" which is what we ask when think we're failing. What we are really asking is, "What's wrong with me?".

Nothing is wrong with your students. Nothing is wrong with you. If you're going along with school as usual, you are all actively participating in a dehumanizing space. Your commitment to your own humanity and theirs, to enact instruction that aligns with your values and responds to their needs, is the most essential component to their success—and yours.

Lesson Plans as Self-Care Plans

Often, we think of lesson planning from a purely intellectual standpoint. We figure out what we want students to know, how they'll show us that they know it, and how they'll come to know it. Constructing learning episodes this way is an intellectual puzzle for us educators that does, indeed, support our self-care. In focusing solely on this area, however, we're missing opportunities to care for ourselves even amidst the "fog of war."

Your lesson plan construction offers you more profound opportunities. If you can think of a lesson plan as a chance to expand your self-care plan, you can convert some of the most challenging tasks and interactions into those which, if not enriching, can at least be less taxing. First acknowledge that you are a whole person as you build and facilitate your lesson plans and then actively manage your physical, social, emotional, and spiritual selves within the lesson plan itself. This can look many different ways which you'll discover as you play with what you need in your own planning process.

Let's explore examples of how your self-care can live in a lesson plan. All of these examples require self-awareness. You'll likely improve as you make this kind of planning conscious, and you'll continue to make seamless, low-energy, high-return improvements as you notice, learn, and adjust.

Physical Self-Care in the Classroom

You don't stop having a body when you walk into your classroom, so you might as well care for it while you're in there. Anything that supports your body to be in healthy, comfortable functioning is physical self-care. An easy way to incorporate physical self-care into your lessons is to focus on times that annoy you or that feel cumbersome. Is it distracting to explain instructions while handing out papers? Put the lesson's printed materials somewhere (or multiple places) in the room so that students can grab them during a transition. Want to sign off on each students' topic sentences before they continue on to write the body of the paragraph, but maneuvering around the room is tough? Sit or stand somewhere in the room and let students bring you their work, which you can approve quickly with a self-inking stamp.

Remember, movement is essential for our physical body. Work movement in wherever you can. When you point to a resource on the wall, do so with your whole arm outstretched, your torso twisting. While students complete their at-the-bell assignments, tuck your arms behind your back, holding your elbows, and stand up straighter. Some physical self-care is lesson-dependent, like building in a plan to move around the room to visit student groups rather than sit at your desk. Some, like deep breathing and stretching, you'll be able to incorporate as habits, no matter the lesson, over time.

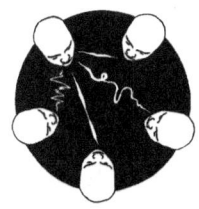

Social Self-Care in the Classroom

Social self-care can show up in a lesson plan in a few ways. Before we explore those, let's reiterate that relying on your students as social equals, is inappropriate. Lesson-plan-embedded social self-care helps you to maintain caring, reciprocal relationships with your students which honor your hierarchically established roles and the rights and responsibilities that come with those roles. You're the teacher; they're the students. And you're all also people. Social self-care in a lesson plan can be strategic self-disclosure. "Instructional use of self " guides sharing with students both authentically and appropriately. For example, as you introduce an activity requiring a certain skill, it might be useful to share an example of how you struggled with a similar skill in your own academic experience and a strategy that helped you overcome that struggle. It would be less useful to disclose that you were afraid that your grandad would hit you if you brought home bad grades.

When we are disclosing as an instructional tool to support a mentoring relationship, our feelings can't dominate. We can do more harm than good if we share our own emotions such that students don't know how to respond or feel concerned about us. Instructional use of self works when "instructional" is prioritized over "self." We know we're caring for our social selves within our lesson plans if we are sharing authentic-but-neutral pieces of information about ourselves to increase connection with students.

Emotional Self-Care in the Classroom

Emotional self-care in a lesson plan requires more self-knowledge, and it involves students less than social self-care. The first step to in-class emotional self-care happens before class begins. Acknowledge how you're feeling about a lesson plan; what parts are you excited about, what parts scare you, which parts are you dreading? Depending upon how you're feeling as you plan each learning episode, intentionally build in ways for that feeling to exist in the room as you facilitate without needing to let your students know what's happening. For example, if I'm nervous about a new activity, naming my nervousness ahead of time allows me to build a backup plan in case the lesson doesn't turn out, which feels better than potentially expressing frustration at students who aren't experiencing the lesson as I hoped they might.

Responding to negative self-talk or fear isn't always efficient or healthy. Another option is to acknowledge the emotion towards disempowering it. It might sound something like, "I think my students have what they need to figure this assignment out, and if they express frustration, I'll focus on the content of their request instead of taking their frustration to mean that the lesson failed." It's okay to say these types of things out loud to our students, too; "I'm excited to try this activity, but it's the first time I've done it with a class this size, so we'll see how it goes." The risk, however, when you acknowledge your emotions with your students, is that you then make them participatory. To retain sovereignty over your emotional realm, own it deeply—so that your emotions don't seep out in harmful ways and so that your feelings aren't levers students can use to pry at your boundaries.

Spiritual Self-Care in the Classroom

Finally, building your spiritual self-care into your lesson plans sounds daunting, but it's much easier than you think. Remember, spiritual self-care connects us to something more important, bigger, and more meaningful than ourselves. Prayer, mantras, and meditation are all excellent tools to support our spiritually connected practice, and they are all privately accessible if our teaching contexts are more outwardly secular. For some of us, our spiritual self-care connects to our values. As long as our values are built into our lesson plans, we have opportunities to connect to meaning while we're teaching.

If we're having a hard time connecting to our values, we can play the "why" game to help us remember that our work matters even when we are asked to work in opposition to our values. Why do these state tests matter? Because I want my students to succeed in navigating frustrating systems to increase their autonomy and choice. Why do I have to teach this content? Because I value learning as a process, and I can focus on process if the content doesn't inspire me. Why do I have to give another benchmark quiz? Because metacognition is never wasted, and I can help students build healthy relationships to feedback processes.

Once I've gone through this exercise, I can ensure that my lesson plan prioritizes messages oriented to my values. I may share these messages with students if the impact is empowerment, not distraction.

Lesson Plans as Student-Care Plans

Your well-being is an essential ingredient for the functioning of your room; your students' well-being is also critically important. Because you're not trained in clinical mental health, you're entirely off the hook for deep, personal, invasive conversations with students (in fact, please don't—please refer to trained clinicians). What better way to rehumanize your instruction than to let students be whole humans within every lesson plan?

Learning is impacted by stress, and stress can be reduced by self-care. It follows that you can minimize student stress in your classroom by incorporating self-care principles in the service of your students. Considering student-care can increase student self-regulation, sense of belonging and investment, and connection to you, your class community, and your content.

Often, when we think about lesson plans, we focus on the intellectual components. This works well for deep, abstract learning in the prefrontal cortex. The trouble is, students don't check their reptilian and mammalian brains at the door. Our whole students bring their whole brains with them. By considering the components for self-care in your lesson planning, you offer students ways to lower stress, connect authentically, and bring their whole selves to your carefully crafted learning episodes.

Lesson plans with embedded self-care principles for students consider the same elements that we keep in mind for ourselves.

Physical Care for Students During Class

To care for students' physically, build in opportunities for students to move. Our attention spans, in minutes, are our ages +10 minutes. We can support students to improve their focus by incorporating more movement. It may suffice to intentionally build in reasons to move (turn in papers, collect and sort materials, etc.) as a part of a transition between activities. For long activities, plan specific breaks. Training your classes in a couple of ways to move when you notice attention lagging is a worthwhile investment that can be fun to figure out with students. Students with mobility issues can be consulted privately about what might work well for them. Everything from standing behind chairs and doing toe-raises, rolling necks and shoulders, and 30-second dance parties in response to a content-centric prompt—all of these activities can support students to stay more connected to their physical selves instead of being distracted by their understandable need to move.

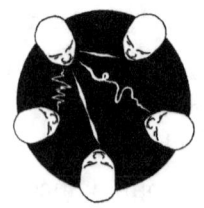

Social Care for Students During Class

The idea of caring for students' social selves can, at first, make educators clench and bristle, particularly if we've been rewarded for enforcing our students' sit-and-stay compliance. Social classroom care is a lot like jiu jitsu; students have the energy regardless, and we're wise to acknowledge that energy by channeling it in learner-supporting ways. Considering students' social well-being in our lesson plans means embedding intentional opportunities for students to interact with each other. The more support we build into our plan, the more we can trust that the interaction will support the neural movement we want. For example, instead of writing "turn and talk" in our lesson plan, which may lead to us saying, "Turn to your partner and tell them what you just learned," and may lead dominant students to over-talk, quieter students to stay quiet, and a whole lot of talk about not-class, we can consider taking more responsibility for the interaction.

Social self-care in lessons can support students to have productive social interactions with each other, as well. Providing clear instructions for expectations around what students are doing with their hands, bodies, and voices (adjusted for grade-appropriateness) can ease social anxiety. Praising the quality of an interaction, or the way students are supporting each other can, in turn, support a social dynamic in the classroom that supports you. Even acknowledging students' social needs and allowing them to be earnestly social during a moment that could otherwise be stressful can add to the social health of the classroom.

The socially-cognizant prompts in our lesson plans clarify what students are doing with their bodies, meter air time, and guarantee every student will have something worthy to contribute. For example, "Partner on the right, look at your partner and share a question you have about the activity we're about to do. Partner on the left, after you wrote your partner's question, look at them and let them know if you have a guess about the answer or if you have that same question. Together, decide two more questions." The clearer you can be about roles, goals, and frames for student interaction, the more successful you'll be at supporting students to use their natural-born urge to connect socially in a way that also connects more dendrites.

Emotional Care for Students During Class

Students' emotions are in the room whether we acknowledge them or not. Emotions are like leftovers: best digested fresh and a bummer if pushed to the back.[55] When students have safe, predict-able ways to access and name their feelings they can be present and focus. Opportunities to name feelings can show up in your starter prompts (e.g. "How are you feeling now that you're back from spring break?" or "How are you feeling about switching the seating plan tomorrow?"). Keep prompts private; we don't want students judging each other in their early moments of emotional self-awareness. We can also make emotions safe by naming them in non-judgmental ways; "It seems like you're frustrated." or, "It's great to see you smile after working so hard. Are you proud of yourself? You deserve to be!"

---

[55] Jacobs Hendel, H. (2018). Ignoring Your Emotions Is Bad for Your Health. Here's What to Do About It. Time Magazine, 27.

Spiritual Care for Students During Class

Finally, supporting students to connect spiritually in the secular space of a public school classroom is easier than you might think. Same as you, all they need to do is connect to something beyond themselves in a meaningful way. Also, there's nothing illegal about acknowledging our membership in faith communities or the importance faith plays in the lives of the faithful. It's possible to allow students' deep meaning seeking into the room, just like it is yours.

For earnest students in spaces more developmentally prone to this kind of connection, sometimes we can help students make meaning (for example: "I know you kindergarteners care about animals. Today, we're going to learn a little bit about plants and how they help animals"). For older or more developmentally advanced students, connecting to their own motivations and meanings can be powerful. For those in developmentally surly stages, offering reasons why other people might care gives a rebellious teenage brain access to why they might care, particularly if they can care in privacy and with some time to digest internally.

You Are A Super Human, But You're Not Superhuman

If you're impacted by structurally oppressive ideas like the Urgency of Everything and the Tyranny of Linear Time, it make senses if this chapter's ideas are overwhelming. Thankfully, because you can trust that you're doing your best, that what you do will be enough, and that your practice is an iterative adventure, you'll be able to sit with these ideas with some spaciousness, some patience, even some curiosity.

Your outside-of-the-classroom self-care plan doesn't require each activity to include each of the five components. Similarly, there's flexibility in how you think about implementing self-care components in your lesson plans. Some lessons will feel less meaningful while some hinge on students connecting with significance beyond themselves. Some days, you will need to interact less, and so you can support your students to interact more. Some days you may need to acknowledge a big feeling that's in the room because of an external event; even though it has "nothing" to do with your plan that day, you can rest easy knowing that acknowledging emotion will allow a return to instruction with students who are can mentally return with you.

Think of self-care in the classroom the same way you do a balanced diet.

There is no way to get every nutrient into every bite. You can't get every self-care component into every lesson. As long as you're mixing it up daily, including each component weekly for both yourself and your students, you're doing great. You're striving for balance, a dynamic condition. You're striving to support yourself, a dynamic being, within a dynamic group of students within a dynamic system. Incorporating self-care components in you classroom will get easier over time.

Student Perception is Student Reality

Self-care principles will work in the classroom is if they work for students, according to students. Students might not feel comfortable telling us that what we're doing isn't working. That's okay. Our data can come from many different components of how a student shows up in our room. Any data is acceptable, if we can accept the data at face value. Structural oppression can foil our attempts at a caring classroom if we let down our guard against our paternalistic parts. If we dismiss student behavior that isn't what we wanted as an inherent student characteristic, or if we think students "should" be able to do things they clearly can't yet do, paternalism is winning.

We can also mess up applying self-care principles as student-care principles by conflating our needs with student needs. Particularly risky in the emotional and spiritual realms, none of this stuff will work for students if we're deciding what the class needs to feel and connect to meaningfully. Our work in acknowledging self-care components in our lesson plans is to make room for these components—explicitly, supportively, and intentionally.

our work is to create the space, not fill it in.

The moment we use our awareness of the importance of emotional processing, for example, to tell students what, when, and how to feel, we have made our classrooms a space in which feeling is an obligation, a punishment, or both. So, too, with meaning-making beyond our content and into the spiritual space. The invitation is for students to make their own connections; we have the honor of supporting those connections as valid, important, and of being allowed to accompany the student whenever and however is meaningful to them.

Too Long; Didn't Read
Chapter 8:
Rehumanize Your Lesson Plans

Ideas

- Rehumanizing your instruction means prioritizing relationships with students in how you conceptualize and facilitate classroom adventures.
- Self-management is the key to values-aligned, effective classroom management.

Strategies

- Acknowledge your values at the start of any goal-setting or instructional planning work by writing them at the top of the page.
- Embed 5 self-care components directly into your lesson plans, for yourself and your students ("intellectual" is considered covered, given the cognitive rigor of facilitating/engaging in worthy instruction).
- In-Classroom Self-Care:
  - Physical – when and how can you move your body?
  - Emotional – build in intentional ways before, during, and after class to acknowledge your complex feelings without needing them to be different and without involving students
  - Social – use self-disclosure wisely for appropriate connection
  - Spiritual – build in intentional ways to connect with your values and a sense of meaning as you develop and facilitate a lesson
- In-Classroom Student Care:
  - Physical – plan safe, cognitively connecting ways for students to move at intervals that will help them stay tuned in for learning
  - Emotional – build in opportunities for students to safely express how they are feeling
  - Social – guide student-to-student interactions to support positive, productive sociality
  - Spiritual – identify opportunities for students to connect to their own senses of meaning safely and explicitly within a learning episode

Chapter 9

Grading as a Remoralizing Practice

In which we explore specific in-classroom instructional strategies to prevent burnout, demoralization, and exploitation.

> *"There is only one thing that makes a dream impossible to achieve: the fear of failure."*
> — Paulo Coelho —

> *"Never limit yourself because of others' limited imagination; never limit others because of your own limited imagination."*
> — Dr. Mae Jemison —

You Are the Expert in Your Context

This is a "brass tacks" type of chapter. Because the goal is to strategize and enact ideas concretely, I'll use concrete examples. When I reference choices I made in my own practice, my goal is simply and solely to offer concrete examples of otherwise abstract ideas. My goal is *not* to tell you what to do. There are as many "right" ways to implement BD&E-preventing ideas as there are practitioners. You know your context the best. You know your strengths, students, limitations, needs, and goals the best. The right way is the way that's right for you, your students, and your life.

So far this book focused on my failure. Let's re-orient. Grading for maximum student learning and minimum practitioner burden is the part of my practice where I found the most healing, liberation, and inspiration. Re-authoring student evaluation was a strength and a joy of mine.

None of the following ideas are revolutionary, nor are they originally mine; they're taught as best practice in every teacher prep program I know of. Unfortunately, however, those methods and curriculum and instruction courses are often taught by practitioners who have not spent substantive time in real-life classrooms, and whose own post-secondary instruction doesn't model the instruction the course encourages. When researchers teach courses for practitioners, the implementation gap widens. When excellent theory is taught in grad school but not modeled in the classrooms where we student-teach, we can't practice what the programs preach. This chapter addresses implementation for pedagogy in which you have likely been trained, but, may not have seen modeled or been able to test-drive.

I offer these approaches from a boots-on-the-ground, practice-based-evidence stance. What follows is not hypothetical. It was an essential part of my practice, and the orientations and actions I offer continue to serve me in supporting adult learners in my present-day practice.

Educators Are Neural Engineers

Because you are reading this book, I assume that you are already an excellent educator. I'm assuming this because you are trying to stay in the classroom so much that, even though you're in pain, you are taking time to read this book towards finding a solution. For that same reason, I am also assuming that a component of your excellence is a commitment to perpetual reflection-driven improvement. Unfortunately, these assumptions don't apply to all educators. Because of the way our profession has been systematically and intentionally devalued, educators are seen—and exist—on a spectrum:

Glorified _____ Neural
Babysitter   Engineer

Even as I write it, "glorified" doesn't seem right. I can't recall a single example of an educator bathed in glory. Perhaps I mean we are perceived as "salaried babysitters." "Glorified" points to how our helper natures are preyed upon; we know we're way more than babysitters, but rather than demand to be treated in accordance with our value, we allow the perspective to persist in exchange for empty rewards like "teacher appreciation week."[56]

Glorified babysitters need only to show up and ensure that no physical harm occurs while a kid's primary caregiver is away.[57] It's precisely this educator-as-babysitter view that leads to phenomena like bullying parents and minimally accountable administrators. The glorified babysitter view neither expects nor supports excellence for students. This view lowers educators' social status, justifying low pay and scripted curriculum mandates.[58] This view drives BD&E. Sadly, teacher-as-glorified-babysitter is also affirmed by the teachers who behave as if babysitting accurately describes their role due to their own burnout, demoralization, and exploitation.

Neural Engineers, on the other hand, understand that their task is to intentionally alter the shape and chemical makeup of their students' brains in order to construct enduring learning to serve that student over a lifetime. Teaching is engineering because we operate within a system driven by goals and limited by constraints in which we have agency to change conditions towards impacting outcomes based on our experience and expertise. I have been assuming, and will continue to assume, that you either already are or strive to be closer to the "neural engineer" side of the educator spectrum as we explore grading, assessment, and evaluation.

Wait—you thought this book was about preventing BD&E, not working harder, right? You're right. If we commit to our roles as neural engineers, working smarter instead of harder becomes a professional mandate instead of a way to "skip out" on what, it turns out, is a ton of ineffectual busywork commonly referred to as "grading." Glorified babysitters grade out of habit, a perfunctory acknowledgement of student activity, and a felt sense of obligation to do something with the assignments students submit. Neural engineers empower students to self-assess towards owning and investing in their own learning process. Neural engineers work smarter, not harder—and their students learn more. Meanwhile, neural engineers grade way, way, way less stuff.

This chapter is written for present-day educators serving in systems

[56] Pasek, B. [@benjpasek]. (2020, May 6). If someone's job requires an appreciation week it means they're not getting paid enough[Tweet]. Twitter.
[57] Vogtman, J. (2017). Undervalued: A brief history of women's care work and child care policy in the United States. National Women's Law Center.
[58] It's messed up to denigrate babysitting (an essential skill and social good), but here I am. Thanks, patriarchy.

resistant to meaningful reform. There are many gorgeous, powerfully worthy visions of what teaching and learning could be if there was visionary administrative and structural support (for a shining example, check out Street Data).[59] This chapter, heck, this whole book, is written for the educator who doesn't have a visionary administrator and who lacks structural support. This is for the educator who needs to function as they implement transformative ideas amidst a recalcitrant culture.

Dendrites Need a Reason to Grow

Learning is a process in which our neurons alter dendritic connections to jettison useless pathways and establish new connections. To motivate enduring learning via persistent neural connections, learners need to interact with a new idea. Ideally, a learner is speaking, writing, drawing, or gesturing about a new idea. Even more ideally, these creative actions are generative instead of simply repetitive. As neural engineers, we know all of this. And sometimes, even though we try our best, we don't meet our design goals.

It's a crushing feeling when you get an exam back. You can tie each question to a specific activity you crafted for the last four weeks of instruction. You know your questions were fair and well-crafted. Yet, some-how, the majority of your students appear to have missed the whole dang point. The first couple of times this happened, my well-meaning colleagues shrugged and offered one of those off-the-cuff, accidentally-professionalizing messages; "Oh, well. Students can't do hard things." Because my own values system couldn't accept that view of students, I started chipping away at why, when I was using every best practice I could, my students were still failing exams on which I had attempted to set them up for success.

The pattern in my room then, and in the classrooms that built us all before we led classrooms of our own, is that we would do an assignment, turn it in, and get it back with a number representing our performance. Those graded assignments sometimes make it back to folders or notebooks but more often end up in the trash.

Students are rational actors. Once my practice embraced this idea, my students' outcomes changed. When I committed to a view of students as

[59] Safir, S., & Dugan, J. (2021). Street data: A next generation model for equity, pedagogy, and school transformation. Corwin.

rational actors, I could no longer blame students for irrational outcomes. I had to reckon with my own engineering; if I'm not getting the behavior and outcomes I'm hoping for, I need to change my incentive structure. Frequently, I also need to have some feelings about it first.

The instance that led to my grading revolution was around a particular lab report. I had spent the entire weekend grading 240 lab reports, handwriting encouraging praise and specific, actionable critique, and relating my comments to the rubric. After first period, I noticed one student had tossed their paper, including my super-thoughtful feedback, into the bin. I took it as a personal offense as I lifted the paper from the bin. But under that paper, full of see-aren't-I-a-thoughtful-teacher comments, there was another paper. And another. Throughout the day, I handed back all 240 papers. Throughout the same day, I saw at least 200 of the papers I had returned in bins in my classroom, the hallway, and even some that were scattered and kicked down the hallway floor.

With every discarded "gift" I discovered, I discovered a bit more resentment. It was big enough that the resentment pushed into my awareness. I wasn't using this language at the time, but I started looking for the boundary that the resentment was pointing to. What was it I thought was going to happen? Why was I so surprised it didn't?

What I wanted was for students to carefully read through my notes, be impressed with the time I had taken to give them such high-quality feedback, save these papers in a folder at home and pull them out to help their next writing assignment. I imagined them to referring back to their papers with comfort and pride during their first collegiate writing adventure. But, why? Why on earth would they do any of that? In a student's overworked world of busywork assignment after busywork assignment, I had handed back something with a final grade on it and with no opportunity for revision, let alone reward for reflection. I hadn't been honest about the contract. I had ignored students' lived incentivization structure. Students had no reason to care. Because I hadn't given them one.

The overwrought lab-feedback adventure revolutionized grading because it pushed me to ask myself—why do I care? As a neural engineer, my task isn't measuring students. It's to support, push, and celebrate them to be able to do more than they did before, and to know that they can.

Neural Engineers Love Failure; Students Can, Too

A wrong answer is the closest thing we have to a portal into our students' brains. Right answers are useless in a neural engineering frame. If a student offers a right answer but offers it for an incorrect reason or based on erroneous reasoning, I won't ever know. I have a false positive; I have a performance of learning without confirmation that learning occurred. If you were brought up by the public education system in the U.S. like I was, you might have the same comfort with (and tendency to seek) right answers that I do. It's a tough habit to break. If enduring learning is our goal, however, right answers are the shortest path to the wrong destination.

When our students offer a wrong answer, we know where to start. Their blue dot pops up on our instructional map, and we've got a way to get them from "there" to "here." This information is directly related to the neuroanatomical shifts in their learning brains—the wrong answer shows us the current shape their brain is in. Each connection we can help them build through questioning and discovery is a "turn" closer to building the enduring dendritic connections we like to refer to as "learning." If failure helps us learn more efficiently, our charge is to not only make it safe to fail in our class-rooms; we have to go much farther than that. In order for failure to be an instructive component of our instruction, students' success needs to depend on their willingness to acknowledge, explore, reflect, and act upon their failures. Our students have to experience failure as a normal, healthy, requisite, public, shame-free part of learning. This is a radical departure from the systems that taught us, from the classrooms where a failing grade meant we were failures as human beings. Thankfully, it's a really easy—and power-fully liberating—shift to make.

How Does Tolerating Failure Help Me Resist BD&E?

If your classroom is built to support, celebrate, and grow from failure (specifically making failure safe, visible, and actionable), your likelihood of BD&E will decrease in several key ways.

You're less likely to burn out because you'll grade less, as you'll be liberated from the paternalistic guilt that compels you to grade everything that your students produce. You will understand how to invite students into evaluation that's more meaningful for them and more efficient for you.

Regarding demoralization, I'm guessing again, here, that nowhere in your list of motivating values did you write, "Reducing students' worth to a score prone to misrepresentation." In that way, a failure-acknowledging classroom culture helps us to resist demoralization as we focus more on process and create incontrovertible evidence that our students are, in fact, learning what we are striving to teach (or if they aren't, we're in dialogue with their process which indicates to us a clear next instructional step).

Finally, a failure-forward classroom can prevent exploitation. Exploitation relies on free labor. Status, as earned through empty recognition, doesn't cost anything and doesn't pay anything. Yet many of us have developed an achievement orientation. Achieving and learning aren't the same thing. A failure-forward classroom acknowledges that there are many correct paths from here to there, that the one working the hardest is the one learning the most, and that all students are deeply capable of rich, meaningful growth. Steeping oneself in that culture is a consistent inoculation against the exploitative tendencies of an oppressive system in which achievement, rather than learning, motivates compliance. We can dodge exploitation by fiercely claiming our roles as facilitators of learning processes, and without over-identifying with learning products.

Learning Requires Cognitive Heavy Lifting

Basic learning science confirms that the one who is talking (or drawing, writing, or gesturing) is the one who is learning. The one evaluating the learner is also learning. When I collect and score a bunch of student work, I get to go through the process of evaluating how close a student was to the ideal answer I had envisioned. If it's a well-designed assignment, I get to see where a student went wrong and what they need to do to course correct. I get to learn what unasked questions could have gotten them to the correct answer sooner, what initial information could have more directly supported their learning adventure. I benefit from all of that. I will always advocate that you stay closely connected to student work.

That said, in the above scenario, I'm the only one who learned all of that stuff from grading that assignment. My students didn't get any benefit. They get a final score that tells them how far from perfect they are. Even when we don't mean to, this approach to grading can confirm a student's fixed mindset (you're born with a set amount of "smarts," it's unchangeable, and showing struggle is admitting you're dumb) vs. encouraging a growth mindset (intelligence is plastic; learning requires productive struggle).[60] Consider the lab report example; my evaluative comments, presented as static facts, only demonstrated how wrong my students were rather than offering them concrete next steps towards improving. I told them they were wrong without offering a chance to get right. If they have no chance to correct the mistakes grading has revealed, I give them no distance between "you failed" and "you are a failure."

Students deserve access to all of that information we get when we grade an assignment. Because they are students, and humans, they need to be supported to know how to use it and incentivized to care.

Process vs. Product

A failure-safe classroom acknowledges that failure is a part of the learning process. This classroom uses a grading scheme which daylights instructional goals, examines products, and offers opportunities to bring products up to meet the standards of the instructional goals.

The quickest way I found to embed failure as an essential component of our classroom was to be explicit with myself about which assignments were "process" assignments and which were "product" assignments. Process assignments aligned with formative assessment; these were the assignments that we would engage in en route, the ways we would access information and construct meaning.[61] I relied process assignments to let me know what my students were understanding and what they needed, and I'd use that info to inform my next instructional decisions. Product assignments are often associated with summative assessments. They're the "how we know they know" final, show-off assignments, like projects or exams. If our failure-safe classroom is empowered and inspired, they're the assignments that make students proud because they understood (via their process assignments) what was expected, what they needed to be able do to meet the expectation, and were able to demonstrate their capacity to meet or exceed the expectation.

---

[60] Dweck, C. (2015). Carol Dweck revisits the growth mindset. Education Week, 35(5), 20-24.
[61] Moss, C. M., & Brookhart, S. M. (2019). Advancing formative assessment in every classroom: A guide for instructional leaders. ASCD.

The following table summarizes a process vs. product grading scheme. In it are artifacts of the systems in which I taught, which required letter grades, used learning management software which required percent out of 100, and didn't include proficiency-based grading options. Before we explore those ideas further, let's look at the way process vs. product lived in my grading scheme specifically, as it helped me to distinguish between the two, both for myself and for my students:

Letter Grade	%	Product vs. Process	Assignment and Interaction Types
A	90-100	**Product:** Assessment OF learning	**Summative**: demonstration of mastery, no chances to re-submit with corrections - Exams - Final Reports - Final Presentations
B	80-89		
C	70-79		
F	0-69	**Process:** Assessment FOR learning	**Formative**: chances to make and correct mistakesakes to build understanding - Daily in-class "journal" activities - Rough draft processes for reports - Exam guides as pre-exam assignments

A student could earn 70% by attending and engaging in class. Of course, I had contingencies for students who needed to be absent, but my goal was to make 99% of both the work and the learning happen during class time, therefore motivating students to attend and minimizing socioeconomic disparities outside of class. My responsibility was to build instructional sequences that, by attending and engaging, students had everything they needed to identify what they understood, what they didn't, and how to gain understanding to demonstrate the level of mastery they wanted to build by the unit's end.

A grading scheme is a numerical embodiment of our values.

Some old-school educators have encountered my scheme and critiqued me roundly for my low expectations. In their eyes, any course in which more than 5% of students are earning an A indicates spineless grade inflation. Respectfully, they are wrong.

This norm-based view argues that only 5% of students are capable of building and demonstrating mastery in any given course. One of my guiding values is in my certainty that all students are capable of learning. I have hundreds of human examples that all humans are capable of some level of content mastery, given sufficient time and support. As an educator, it's my job to help them to build said mastery, not simply score them according to an elitist scale that quantifies the number of personal and cultural barriers they've faced and pretend I'm scoring their "innate" intelligence.

Just because in my classroom or any classroom, anyone who showed up, completed work, and demonstrated mastery could earn an A does not mean that earning that A was easy. Earning an A required tons of attempts, critiques, and corrections. I wasn't giving anything away by making these learning processes an explicit part of my classroom. I was simply acknowledging that they are requisite components of learning, and supporting them for all of my students. Instead of expecting students to know how to be learners on their own time, in their outside-of-school worlds, I brought the entire arc of learning into my classroom. I was acting in alignment with my values, as the enduring beliefs that all students are both capable and deserving of rich, challenging learning experiences and mastery-via-self-determination are core to my worldview as an educator.

According to this scheme, when students completed assignments during class, they got full credit. If this was carte blanche, full credit for scribbles on the paper, this would have been grade inflation—or, at least, a room full of "C" students. Rather, the process for which they earned credit included the completion, evaluation, and reflection on in-class assignments and activities. For example, after data collection during a lab, students would individually write a first draft of a paragraph interpreting their results. They would then share with their "elbow partner," and adjust their paragraph if their understanding shifted. To scaffold students to construct meaning correctly along the way, I would then share three content-related questions their paragraph should answer. If necessary, students would discuss in small groups, then add, correct, or expound upon their paragraph to ensure that they were answering the content questions. Finally, they would indicate if they were unsure of their answers and wanted me to triple-check them.

Students turned in their process-oriented writing, and I entered full-credit for all those which were complete (and a scaled amount of credit— 50% complete = 50% credit, a marker in the grade book of an incomplete process assignment that can be completed up to one week before the final). I'd respond to those who were unsure, sometimes directly, but often by addressing the whole class. This allowed me to be less susceptible to high-concern students' perpetual "am I right?" anxiety while still supporting students to develop accurate understandings.

Rapid-fire feedback on process assignments can be even more immediate. As a science teacher, much of my work was supporting students in conceptualizing invisible processes. We drew lots and lots of models. I would put a model's criteria on the board; "Model the difference between ice, liquid water, and steam. Include a key to identify water molecules, molecular charges, and energy. Each accurate component earns one stamp for a total of 3 possible stamps." With this approach, I could zip around the 40+ person room to the raised hands, take four to five seconds per student to look, stamp using my handy personalized self-inking stamp, and let the student know what was correct and what needed adjusting. I could build students up by quietly confirming their right answers, and ask, if I sent other students to them, they'd be able to explain their drawing instead of simply silently offering it to peers to copy. I could then send specific students to specific other students (ex: "If you're confused about how to represent energy, you could ask Irving and Deja for two excellent examples!").

Self and Peer Evaluation: Improve Learning and Prevent BD&E

The surest way to engage students in self and peer evaluation is to build it into the structure of your class. If you're uncomfortable with this idea (anything from "they'll cheat" to "they'll just confirm each other's wrong answers"), rest assured; you can address those problems. What's more, you can trust that any time you trust your students to support each other in learning, even if they're discussing something incorrectly, their likelihood of constructing enduring learning is actually improving.[62]

For students to trust the room enough to evaluate themselves and each other, we have to incentivize honesty more than they've already been incentivized to seek points at all costs. For example, let's take a quiz. If I just ask students to swap papers and grade each other as I read out answers, I've

---

[62] Tullis, J. G., & Goldstone, R. L. (2020). Why does peer instruction benefit student learning? Cognitive Research: Principles and Implications, 5(1), 1-12.

created a whole bunch of opportunities for bummer things to happen. Not only have I invited a power dynamic primed for bullying, I've incentivized being right. In the usual mark-your-answers-wrong-if-they're-wrong-and-lose-points-if-they're-wrong approach, students can choose between being honest or earning points. And neither choice addresses learning. If I want students to utilize feedback for enduring dendritic motion, I need to incentivize students to interpret and respond to feedback.

Peer grading incentivizes learning when it emphasizes and rewards acknowledging and correcting our mistakes and misunderstandings. For peer grading of quizzes (a classroom practice that I noted in my course disclosure and syllabus to manage parent expectations), students had important roles as evaluators and feedback recipients. Both roles were explicitly acknowledged and reciprocal. Students would trade papers and put their own writing utensils under their seats. They'd use a class set of feedback pens (I liked purple); feedback pens were necessary the first two or three rounds of peer grading, as students didn't yet trust that they wouldn't be penalized for wrong answers. Together as a class, we'd walk through the questions and review answers.

True, the feedback pens minimized cheating. The goal wasn't so much to prevent cheating, however, but rather to offer behavioral support for students as they learned a new approach. At the top of their peer's paper, they'd write "feedback from (their name)." The evaluating student marked the answers that required correction, then they'd return each other's quizzes. Each student would then write a brief reflection about what they'd missed, why, and what they need to do to answer correctly, and then they'd put their own process grade at the top (ex: four questions missed, four reflection statements written = 100%). This is the grade that gets recorded. In this way, the benefit of cheating is minimized. This is particularly true if your assignments relate to your assessment such that cheating on a quiz by saying you understood something that you didn't understand reliably leads to a lower score on a final exam.

Did you catch the part where, because we took class time to evaluate an assignment together, I didn't have to grade...*anything*??? Students engaged in the assignment as I would want any excellent, self-motivated, culturally-savvy student to do, but I didn't have to depend on any student's pre-built sense of excellence, self-motivation, or cultural savviness to ensure that they did. Nor did I have to rely on them having these things outside of class, or the addition of a U.S.-educated, English-speaking parent around with enough free time to "help" with homework. I am addressing opportunity gaps by ensuring that our time in class together is opportunity enough to excel. And I can enter the whole class as scoring 100%, flip through the pile in approximately three minutes (for a class of 40), and adjust any grades that didn't earn full credit. Maximum impact on student learning, minimum time I spend writing check marks and circling proportions at the tops of pages.

Want to know how many of those types of assignments I've found in the recycling bin? I'd be lying if I told you zero, but I can confidently say that it's less than 2%. More importantly, student outcomes improved I started sharing evaluative processes instead of martyring myself to grading.

"Because It's Easier to Grade" Isn't Values-Aligned Rationale

For the smarter-not-harder approach to grading to work, a couple of things have to be true. Most importantly, ease in grading for you cannot be the primary motivation behind your grading plans. In fact, when "it's easier to grade" is the answer a practitioner offers, particularly without any other pedagogical consideration, I'm immediately concerned that they're being impacted by burnout, and that their burnout may be impacting their students.

If a decrease in our grading load leads to an increase in students' experience of "busywork," performative assignment completion, or non-learning, then we've prioritized ourselves over our students' experience. Decisions like these help us add demoralization to our own burnout, as they rarely support our practice to align more closely with our values.

Group projects, particularly those with group grades, are an excellent example of how managing a grading scheme for educator ease undermines other instructional goals. I get it—asking students to pair up means I would only have to read 20 lab reports instead of 40. If they're working in quads, I only have to read 10 per class! The thing is, if I couple the decision to ask students to work in groups with the effort required to minimize the bummer dominant-culture dynamics which so reliably make group work terrible for everyone involved, then I end up doing just as much work in setting the group work up for success as I would grading 40 individual lab reports.[63] If I don't do that extra work, I'm actively selecting a spot on the "glorified babysitting" end of the spectrum. Well-supported group work is an essential part of an enriching learning experience, and it requires significant preparation and attention from the instructor. Inadequately supported group work is easy to facilitate and a great way to save your time by wasting your students' time.

We're allowed to shift the evaluation process—and workload—over to students if doing so:
- supports a cooperative learning environment
- encourages trying-and-failing-and-trying-again
- allows students to more fully own their own learning process, and
- offers students a "next step" opportunity to correct errors they discover (without authoring negative stories about themselves or their capacities).

When filtered through these criteria, the group work from the previous paragraph wouldn't pass muster. "But," you may protest, "students have to learn to work in groups!" Often when we say this, what we're really saying is, "Students have to learn that working in groups sucks, and is an inevitable component of the conglomerate disappointment of adulthood, and the sooner you get with that, the better. Especially if I have to grade less stuff." If, however, being an assertive, flexible, kind, contributory member of a group is a skill set we value building in students, then assertive, flexible, kind, contributory group membership is what our grading structure must incentivize.

You Don't Have to Grade Everything—Or Do You?

You don't have to grade everything.

For those of us who are particularly sensitive to an imagined sense of external accountability, the pressure to grade everything can feel very real. It's not. You can let it go.

If there are things you're open to leaving ungraded, however, they are

---

[63] Lotan, R. A., & Holthuis, N. I. (2021). Complex instruction for diverse and equitable classrooms: In loving memory of Elizabeth G. Cohen. In N. Davidson (Ed.), Pioneering perspectives in cooperative learning (pp. 63-77). Routledge.

worth an examination. If they are activities worth doing, particularly from a constructivist perspective, then there is likely some valuable formative assessment data in every assignment. Leaving this data un-accessed, either by yourself or your students, may be wasteful. It may also have a negative secondary impact; if students perceive that they are doing work that is not evaluated, they will increasingly frame work in a context of "matters" vs. "doesn't matter." If you are asking students to complete work that matters, but you don't want to grade it, consider how you'll communicate to your students that it does matter in an incentivizing way (telling them "this really matters even though I'm not going to look at it nor enter it in the grade book" isn't going to cut it).

If you're finding yourself filling time with in-class activities that you don't' know how to evaluate, particularly because you're unsure about why you're facilitating them or how they connect to your learning objectives as measured by your summative assessments, consider letting them go. Less is more when it comes to grading, particularly regarding what students can learn from activities and evaluations. One well-crafted focal activity that invites well-facilitated student self and peer feedback will get you more dendritic growth than four super-cute, Pinterest-worthy activities that your students enjoy but cannot connect to other content, let alone learning self-awareness or meaning-making. We have to actively push against external pressure to urgently "cover" more content. We have to insist on process over product, knowing, of course, that well-supported processes are the only reliable route to products that are worth a damn.

Timing Matters

There are likely unavoidable "crunch" times in your academic year. Even if you do a great job shifting from grading to student metacognition through self-evaluation, you're still the teacher of record and must be the final authority on summative student assessments. And you'll want to be. Student data is always instructive about how you'll change an activity or unit, and those summative moments can also be opportunities to connect individually with students about their goals and progress. This kind of grading can take time. When, exactly, you need to grade is a choice you have more power over than the academic calendar may lead you to believe.

A colleague of mine used to manage the science fair for her district. Technically, she was probably paid, but I'm sure it worked out to approximately $0.02 per hour when averaged across the time she invested. The timing of the district fair always landed in mid-February to be held in time to tally results and announce the winners, who would proceed to the next level of competition. Her partner's birthday also fell in mid-February. For two decades, this human was unavailable for her partner's birthday.

I don't offer the above story out of judgment but out of heartbreak. It's my own heartbreak, as I think this couple did what worked for them, and it's certainly not my business to judge their choices. The heartbreak is in knowing that educators are making similar decisions about high-stakes trade-offs across the country. For those with partnerships facing different demands, that kind of trade-off can be relationship ending. I offer the story as another example of how, if unchallenged, the gig will keep taking. I can't help but wonder what would have happened if this practitioner had drawn a line and unapologetically, with resolve and without explanation, scheduled the science fair one week earlier. Other educators may have pushed back, parents may have tantrumed. But, after the first year, they would have figured it out. And she would have had 20 years of celebrating her partner on their birthday.

Things will inevitably come up that will force us to put our professional obligations ahead of our personal ones—once in a while. Your responsibility is to acknowledge how many of those times, if you had been willing to build your whole self into your planning and acknowledged the actual time a task requires, were actual unforeseen emergencies vs. preventable crunches. No matter how efficient we get, the workload will still be significant and inevitable. The timing and execution of the workload is more variable than we're trained to consider, and this difference can mean everything.

It's okay to make a final assignment due a week before the end of the term so that you can grade a few each day during your prep period and get your grades entered in time without your own kid having to skip dance class that week because you were too swamped to give them a ride. It's okay to change the order of lessons from wonderful to okay-but-less-ideal if it means you'll have a mellower lesson to facilitate the Monday you return from a stressful weekend with extended family. Focusing your grading on only a portion of an assignment is okay. Again—it's never okay to cut corners because you've given up (burnout), particularly in ways that harm students. It is, however, an excellent idea to be honest about how hard your job is, compassionate to yourself as you consider how you'll support yourself to do your job well, and realistic about the tiny tweaks that will, on balance, help you to be more present and pleasant for your students during your 180 days together.

Too Long; Didn't Read
Chapter 9:
Grading as a Remoralizing Practice

Ideas

- You are the expert in your context; own your autonomy and expertise wherever you can.
- You don't have to grade everything.
- How you grade can minimize your workload, maximize student learning, and build authentic classroom community.

Strategies

- Allowing students to participate in setting and evaluating grading criteria decreases your workload and increases their cognitive engagement.
- Celebrate failure without penalizing by using your grading scheme to support students to learn from their mistakes.
- Trust students to evaluate themselves and each other, and set them up for success to do so.
- Schedule projects, exams, and other significant grading demands in a way that works for you and your life, as well as for instructional flow and district calendar constraints.

Chapter 10

To Teach to Live, Live to Teach

In which we acknowledge that you are a world-class change agent, a role which impacts your whole life, and we find ways to build your whole life to support your teaching while minimizing teaching's negative whole-life impacts.

"Though you can love what you do not master,
you cannot master what you do not love."
— Mokokoma Mokhonoana —

Teaching Is Lovable

All of the approaches offered in this book will feel more possible if we make another shift; what if you aren't doing this work to survive teaching, but because you love it?

We've affirmed that teaching is hard. We'll keep affirming that, because it will keep being true. What we have emphasized less, but what deserves just as much emphasis, is that you love it. There are parts of the gig that work well for you on every level. Supporting young humans to keep becoming humans is meaningful and nourishing. Even in contexts of the most controlled curriculum, we have freedom over how we interact with students. Many other jobs include more frequent and intense supervision. And it's not only ok but important to admit how good it is for our quality of life to be guaranteed holidays with our families and summers away from the classroom.

We can love teaching without letting it own our entire identity and damage our lives. Counter-intuitively, we save ourselves and our love for teaching by allowing teaching to inform our entire identity. By joyfully, emphatically, and non-apologetically owning our choice to teach, we can live our lives fully—including our choice to teach, not in spite of it.

Teaching Is A Big Deal

To better understand what it means to choose to build an identity around an activity that is hard, lovable, and worthy, let's use an analogy. Through a series of complete coincidences, as no part of my life overlaps with extreme athleticism, a friend of mine is a world-class endurance athlete.[64] As in, a clocking the fastest known time of a trail-less ridge line route through a 100-mile mountain range in a sleepless 48-hours of unsupported running kind of athlete. I emphasize the randomness of this because I, to be clear, am not one of those. Though many of his friends are also athletes, so few are capable of his level of performance that it's hard for them to participate with him. Because we love and admire him, but can't join in a significant part of his world, the second-best thing we can do is to support him in whatever ways he needs to structure his life to be able to continue doing those things.

In this analogy, I am not comparing you to Sunday joggers (no shade, Sunday joggers). I am comparing you to a super-athlete, to someone whose chosen activity is so grueling and all-encompassing that a lot of their energy when they're not doing that thing is still about that thing.

I'm comparing educators to world-class athletes on purpose. This metaphor is meant to affirm that teaching is both hard and worthy. Teachers interact with an astonishing number of humans, and each interaction is rich with opportunities for deep connection. Teachers are asked to shoulder a wide range of sociocultural expectations, often while insufficiently supported. Teachers are creative powerhouses, generating more new ideas in a given week than professionals in other fields are invited to within their entire careers. The only other professionals who make more decisions per unit time are air traffic controllers; educators make an average of 1500 decisions per day—according to research completed before smartphones were a thing.[65] Teachers are a big deal. *You Are a Big Deal*.

The bummer for educators is that, even though You Are a Big Deal, you're the only one you can rely on to consistently behave like that is true.

---

[64] He's a "run to live," contributory community member, not a "live to run" self-actualizer, for the record.

[65] Jackson, P. W. (1990). Life in classrooms. Teachers College Press.

The good news is that acting like You Are a Big Deal is enough. Once you claim extreme self-care as your responsibility, it's easier for it to live in all parts of your life so that you can participate in your life more fully.

The most crucial analogy in this athlete-to-educator comparison is how big of a deal you are. The second most important part is how okay his big-dealedness is for the people in my friend's life who love and support him. No one in his life is bothered by how he needs to live to support his life-affirming choices. His dietary preferences are honored, his getting up to stretch a calf in the middle of a meal doesn't raise an eyebrow. He goes to bed early, naps, makes weird requests at restaurants and doesn't apologize; he realizes that, to perform at the level he does, his personal life will inevitably be informed by his need for extreme self-care. He's not only allowed to care for himself toward excellence, he's socially supported to do so.

You are responsible for knowing what you need to do in order to do what you want to do. If you tell that to the important people in your life and they support you, excellent! If you find yourself constantly apologizing for what you need to people who claim to care about you, that is concerning. Secure relationships don't tolerate each other's boundaries, they celebrate them.

Decisions Are Expensive

The English word "decide" has the same Latin lineage as "homicide." When we make a decision, we kill at least one of two options. This intense reality is amplified for people who make an extraordinary number of decisions during their standard work day.

As an educator, you are particularly susceptible to decision fatigue, a sub-type of burnout. Technically, decision fatigue describes how humans make worse choices after having to make many choices.[66] This certainly applies to educators, and seems to go one step further in that not only do we make worse decisions (like all humans with predictably fallible and exhaustible brains), but the task of making a decision in the first place begins to feel overwhelming.

Decision fatigue is inevitable. We won't ever be free of it. There will never be fewer decisions that must be made in real-time when facilitating a room full of real humans. If you're sensitive to characteristics of White

---

[66] Tierney, J. (2011). Do you suffer from decision fatigue? The New York Times.

supremacy like perfectionism or a perpetual sense of urgency, decisions become even more stressful. Having accepted this, we can then intentionally set ourselves up to have the energy and presence of mind for the decisions that really matter. Because we can't change our limited capacity for decision-making, the best we can hope to do to decide *what we're going to decide about.* We set ourselves up to decide well about decisions we care about by protecting ourselves against the types of decisions we care about less.

Decide When You're Strong

Our decision-making day begins the moment we wake in the morning. Immediately, we're greeted with an onslaught of potential decisions. Should we push snooze? Do we want to let the dog out before or after we pee? Is that creamer still okay to put in the coffee? Individually, each are inconsequential questions. Our brains, however, don't experience them as separate. Re-member, decision fatigue is the cumulative stress impact of needing to decide many things over time.

Free your brain for the decisions that matter by making decisions ahead of time about as many choices as possible.

We can decide ahead of time about the to-snooze-or-not-to-snooze decision by putting the alarm across the room. By making it harder to hit the snooze button in general, we stack the situation in our favor by choosing, ahead of time, to get out of bed every morning. If mornings are particularly rough, we may put a second alarm even further from the bedroom. By the time we turn off the alarm(s), we have to make a more conscious decision to return to bed than to keep going with our day. We decide, when we're rested and strong, that getting up on time is the right decision, and so we build our morning to support it. That's one less real-time decision we have to make.

Reliable routines minimize decision-making and maximize efficiency. Committing to an order in your habit cascade will help you complete the same repetitive tasks efficiently without using any precious decision-making energy for them.[67] For example, if letting the dog out is on the way to the bathroom as I wake up in the morning, I'd let the dog out first. If the bathroom is between here and the back door, I'd pee first. By deciding that I will routinize the order of these two tasks once, I don't have to decide

---

[67] Clear, J. (2018). Atomic habits: An easy & proven way to build good habits & break bad ones. Avery.

about the order each morning. We can look for demand-lowering pre-choices everywhere. The creamer, for example; we can get smaller containers of creamer and adjust the fridge temperature to eliminate the in-the-moment decision demand of evaluating your morning beverage freshness.

It's ok if these examples don't apply to your life. The point is not to tell you what to do, it's to offer a framework to evaluate your own context and apply decision-demand-reducing principles in ways that work for you.

When asked about decision fatigue, neuroscientist Oliver Sacks replied, "I don't have the problem... I make a willful choice that certain things I care about a lot and I worry over, and then there's a whole swath of my life that I just don't choose."[68] For the majority of his adult life, Dr. Sacks' nightly meal consisted of a bowl of tabouli and a tin of sardines. Do you need to learn to love tabouli and sardines to have a sane career in the classroom? Nope! I offer this example because Dr. Sacks is someone to take seriously; he could have afforded anything for any meal, but he understood that no matter how wealthy or successful, he couldn't purchase more decision-making capacity. It was valuable enough to him to save his decision-making for important decisions that he was willing to let dinner not be one of them. Taking decision fatigue seriously means ruthlessly addressing the parts of your life where you're wasting your decision-making power.

You have already taken a step in fighting your own decision fatigue. You have decided to put things onto your calendar in a way that gives you the space, time, and unpressured freedom to consider, weigh options, and factor in what's most important to you. You've already decided what you value ahead of time. The trick now is to make as many daily decisions as possible as automated as possible to free your brain to manage the parts of life—and teaching—that are harder to predict.

Routine Frees Your Brain

Eliminating unnecessary uncertainty does great things for all three major parts of our brain; it helps us feel safe and secure while freeing critical decision-making space. You already know the power of routine for your students. Embracing your own routines in a way that feels liberating instead

---

[68] Abumrad, J, Krulwich, R. (Hosts). (2002-2020). Radiolab [How Much is Too Much?]. WNYC Studios. https://www.wnycstudios.org/podcasts/radiolab/segments/91641-how-much-is-too-much

of confining is also a key component of your extreme self-care.

If we aren't intentional, routines may or may not emerge. If they do, it's likely our routines aren't as efficient as they could be, or they include features that might not serve us. During my darkest year in the classroom, I was in the middle of a depressive episode. Getting out of bed felt herculean, and I cried (about nothing? everything?) from the time I woke up until I parked before heading into school for the day.

My "routine" during this time was to push snooze six times, run around the house yelling "Crap, crap, crap..." as I frantically showered and convinced myself that I didn't need to eat, jump in the car, realize halfway to work that I was actually really hungry, drive through McDonalds for a hashbrown, and tumble into class a few minutes before the first bell. Thankfully, my in-class routine was less susceptible to my overwhelmed state, so I never left without knowing what I was doing the next day, but man. I sure did make mornings more stressful for myself than I needed to.[69]

When I was in better balance, my morning routine started the night before. I would come home, exercise, and eat dinner. While eating, I would look at my planner for the next day and list anything out-of-the-ordinary I needed to remember to pack, deciding what clothing would make sense, checking the weather to confirm my departure time. I would lay out my clothes, pack my lunch, and gather everything for my work bag before I went to sleep. I prepped my mug with an unwrapped tea bag, filled the kettle, and grabbed a homemade muffin (chocolate with zucchini, carrots, and cabbage – this will make more sense soon) from the freezer to defrost in the toaster oven over night. In the morning, all I had to do was fumble through clicking the kettle on (which I could have even further routinized by getting a cheap outlet timer), showering, and stepping into the outfit I had already decided on. While I still usually ate breakfast en route, the difference between this and the previous scenario I offered minimized both my decision-making energy and my pre-workday stress.

Often, people build routines for the things they want to do. It can also be useful to routinize the things that you aren't excited about precisely so that you can think about them less. For example, build a new routine in

---

[69] Depression is real, and no routine alone can combat depression's physiological impacts. If you're struggling, please access the care you deserve with the support of a clinical mental health professional.

which you load or unload the dishwasher for 5 minutes every morning while your warm beverage heats up. Don't think about it every morning. Instead, just decide once that you'll routinize it, and then build the habit. If you notice that you're stressed in the morning because you can't find your keys, give a gift to your future self by installing a key hook and practice walking in and hanging up your keys first thing. Still lose your keys? Invest in an app-connected tracker. No judgement. Make all the demand-lowering, decision-fatigue-preventing pre-decisions you need to. Your invitation is to keep your number of decisions and stress from decision making as low as possible, when and however possible.

Control What You Can, No Matter How Small

When we learn to tolerate less-than-ideal circumstances in one area of our life, it's tempting to lower our standards across the board. It requires less decision-making. The problem is that educators can be spartan. We can tolerate conditions that are much rougher than they need to be for much longer than is reasonable, often for no good reason. Reclaiming your self-care means examining your ability to tolerate pain.

Because there will always be more urgent-feeling demands on your time, taking the time to care for yourself by removing barriers and attention drains in your environment can seem trivial. That's because you're accustomed to triaging. You're good at letting the small things go. The trouble with people who are used to over-triaging is that once we've categorized something as less important than the present emergency, we then act like it's not ever important. All of a sudden, it's next summer and the vacuum is still broken, we're still holding our coffee cup weirdly to avoid the chip, and we're still not wearing half of our pants because they still aren't hemmed. Being spartan can be a tool. If we hold it right, it can also be a self-harming weapon

While sometimes requisite for survival, tolerating an unnecessarily unkempt and chaotic personal world sends a consistent, subtle message to you that you're not worth taking care of. And that is the opposite of the truth. Sometimes living in alignment and honoring your worth means taking care of the most menial things. Deciding not to care about something that is bothersome still requires decision-making energy. Your work is too important to be impacted by small things that you don't actually have to tolerate, particularly if you build a way to avoid spending much decision-making energy on fixing them.

You are empowered to improve your immediate environment. If there are things that aren't working for you, figure out what's changeable, and change it.

It takes both time and effort to be responsible
for your own experience of your life.

That's okay. We can protect that time like you've learned to do for other facets of your self-care plan. Once per quarter, for example, set time aside to manage things that annoy you, that demand brain space in a non-urgent way. Even just one hour. If, in that hour, you schedule a plumber to look at that faucet, sew the missing button back on your jacket, or file down the rough part on the gate that keeps catching on your bag? Now you get to stop thinking about those things for a long, long time. Any mental space you can free up is a win.

Love Your Brain, Love Your Microbiome

During my third year teaching, I planned to attend a Friday 4:15 p.m. yoga class with a colleague. We thought it was a perfect plan; the class was late enough to wrap up after our Friday classes, early enough to still do other things with the rest of the evening, and, most importantly, we would motivate each other to actually do it. The first week, however, she couldn't make it. We didn't go the second week, either. Eventually, I asked directly— are you not digging this idea? She felt terrible about bailing, and she was embarrassed to admit that the reason she couldn't make 4:15 Friday yoga was because her guts wouldn't let her. Every week, she was spending five days out of seven in a state of intestinal distress that not only increased her in-the-moment stress, but also likely impacted her brain chemistry and general sense of well-being. In her commitment to being an excellent teacher, she had denied herself permission to figure out what worked for her in a fundamental space in her life—her microbiome.

Your microbiome, the trillions of bacteria you cart around in your intestines every day, matters.[70] In addition to communicating with many

---

[70] Schroeder, B. O., & Bäckhed, F. (2016). Signals from the gut microbiota to distant organs in physiology and disease. Nature Medicine, 22(10), 1079-1089.

other organs, a well-worn neural pathway goes from your gut to your brain. It has a significant impact on your mental health, particularly regarding the chemicals involved in depression and anxiety.[71] The bulk of your body's serotonin, the hormone responsible for stabilizing our mood and promoting feelings of well-being and happiness, is produced in our gut (a process that is inhibited when we take SSRI-type anti-depression drugs).[72] However, as foods have gotten more and more processed, we're growing populations of gut bacteria that don't always support the most functional brain chemistry. Thankfully, it doesn't take much to change the composition of our microbiome; we just need to increase the amount and diversity of the plants we eat.[73]

Your microbiome and your regularity are not functionally related within your gut, but they're behaviorally related, as far as we're concerned; both are supported by an increase in fiber consumption. Teachers are tempted to eat a bunch of processed foods because we're both under perpetual stress and so dang busy all of the time; stress increases our craving for processed foods, and business increases the appeal of convenience for a snack less likely to spoil. While the cravings are real, at a certain point, the justification for eating food we can get at any gas station is absolute bologna.

It takes as much time to eat a bag of chips as it does a carrot. Or an apple. Or a handful of almonds. If you really insist that you're too busy to eat plant fiber, a mediocre substitute is a drinkable fiber (better than nothing, will help regularity), but the consequence of that choice is in your microbiome's limited access to different kinds of fiber. We care about fiber diversity because we care about microbiome diversity. We can grow a more diverse microbiome by eating a broader diversity of plants, as each species of plant offers our microbiome a slightly different fiber to snack on. A more diverse microbiome leads to happier brain chemistry.

If it's hard to eat things you aren't craving, consider switching how you think about eating fruits and vegetables. If you think of the task as an

[71] Clapp, M., Aurora, N., Herrera, L., Bhatia, M., Wilen, E., & Wakefield, S. (2017). Gut microbiota's effect on mental health: The gut-brain axis. Clinics and Practice, 7(4), 131-136.

[72] Fung, T. C., Vuong, H. E., Luna, C. D. G., Pronovost, G. N., Aleksandrova, A. A., Riley, N. G.,... Hsiao, E. Y. (2019). Intestinal serotonin and fluoxetine exposure modulate bacterial colonization in the gut. Nature Microbiology, 4, 2064-2073.

[73] Deehan, E. C., & Walter, J. (2016). The fiber gap and the disappearing gut microbiome: implications for human nutrition. Trends in Endocrinology & Metabolism, 27(5), 239-242.

ongoing commitment to your mental health, one that doesn't need to upend any of your other eating habits, it's easy to add an extra orange here and an extra bell pepper there. If there's a choice between peanut butter and a multi-seed option, get the multi. If you wouldn't notice throwing some sprouts on your sandwich, toss a pinch of them in there. The goal is to eat as many different types of plants as consistently as possible.

Sleep Is Art and Science

The most valuable thing you can do for your sanity in your classroom and your quality of life outside of it is to attend to your sleep hygiene.[74] Sleep is our brain's time to repair cellular damage and process all of the information it receives during the day. The rest of our body also repairs while we slumber. While sleep remains a complex and little-understood phenomenon, there's no debate regarding its essential role in brain health. Sleep directly impacts mental health, emotional health, and cognitive functioning. Sleep is a big deal. You are a big deal. This works out!

The practice of curating a consistent and healthy sleeping routine is called sleep hygiene. We currently understand sleep hygiene to include the following key features:

- **Duration**—How much sleep people need is widely variable. If you have never been able to sleep for eight hours, and that's a source of stress because you think you're supposed to, it might not matter as much as you worry that it does. That said, eight hours remains the norm for a healthy amount of sleep, and it's a good idea to protect the time to support that. If you need more than eight hours per night, you best protect more than eight hours per night.

- **Timing**—Going to sleep at the same time each evening and waking at the same time each morning is essential. It takes four nights of standard duration to catch up on one missed hour.

- **Task Isolation**—Your bed is for sex and sleep only. No grading. Reading only if it helps you sleep, and as few screens as possible (see below). Keeping this strict boundary supports your body's circadian rhythm to

---

[74] Irish, L. A., Kline, C. E., Gunn, H. E., Buysse, D. J., & Hall, M. H. (2015). The role of sleep hygiene in promoting public health: A review of empirical evidence. Sleep Medicine Reviews, 22, 23–36.

interpret environmental cues to support the change in metabolism and hormone production necessary for sleep.

- **Device Management**—Phones, tablets, and computers interrupt our sleep cycles in two key ways: in addition to their ability to activate our fight-or-flight responses as we field emails and texts, they also produce ultraviolet or UV light (which is also called "blue" light).
  To combat the impact of devices on your ability to rest deeply, keep them out of your room. If you use your phone as an alarm, plug it in across the room, ensuring that notifications are silenced. In addition to keeping devices out of the bedroom, consider blue light blocking filters on your devices or glasses. The blue light emitted by screens tricks our brains into thinking it's daytime, ensuring that we miss out on those circadian cues to prep our bodies for sleep.

- **Lighting**—Our brains are sensitive to light both as we prepare to sleep and during sleep itself. Consider attending to the lighting in your bedroom. Light bulbs that emit a warm, amber glow support our brains in knowing it's time to wind down. Look for bulbs with a color temperature of 2700k or less. Anything over 3000k will start approximating daylight, which won't help your brain to transition to sleep.

To support high-quality, uninterrupted sleep, ensure no artificial light is present in your bedroom. Pitch black is ideal. This can be achieved with a sleep mask, light-blocking curtains, etc. Motion-sensing, warm amber nightlights are a good way to stay safe if you need to go to the restroom without turning on lights and messing up your sleep-supporting brain chemistry.

Consider Therapy

There's nothing wrong with you. You should still consider therapy.

You've heard the expression "hurt people hurt people"? Throughout the course of your career, you're going to hang out with many people, most of them in tender, impressionable developmental moments in their own lives. Because you're a person, you have likely already encountered challenging circumstances, and you may continue to. There is a strong likelihood that, should you wish to leave components of your experience unconsidered, your own personal pains, assumptions, misinterpretations, and best-you-could-at-the-time worldview may harm your students. Even if none of that is true for you, the truth is that teaching alone is challenging. All educators deserve support. Including you.

Beyond the fact that you deserve support, support may benefit you more than it might a non-helping professional. We who choose helping professions tend to have a much higher rate of developmental trauma than the general population.[75] This means that when we were most dependent on other people, we may have been victims of neglect and/or abuse at higher rates than people who choose careers like accounting or hedge fund management. Because we also know that those who suffer abuse are more likely to behave in abusive ways in their own lives, this means that seeking support isn't just for our own well-being. We need to consider healing for the benefit of all of the people in both our personal and professional lives.

Can't afford therapy? Check into your district health insurance, which usually offers 6–10 free sessions as a part of an employee-assistance program. Grab a group of colleagues you trust and ask a practitioner to facilitate a support group. Hop online to any of the hundreds of thousands of free online support groups happening at any time for a variety of mental health challenges. Read a book that may help you conceptualize yourself and your relationship to your self-concept, emotions, and relationships. What you do may be less important than your simple commitment to do something to ensure that you don't put your "stuff" on your students.

---

[75] Bryce, I., Pye, D., Beccaria, G., McIlveen, P., & Du Preez, J. (2023). A systematic literature review of the career choice of helping professionals who have experienced cumulative harm as a result of adverse childhood experiences. *Trauma, Violence, & Abuse, 24*(1), 72-85.

Too Long; Didn't Read
Chapter 10:
To Teach To Live, Live to Teach

Ideas

- You love teaching. Many parts of the job work really well for you.
- Teaching feels hard because it is hard. Treat your brain the way an athlete would treat their body, and use your out-of-classroom choices to support your in-classroom capacity.
- Decisions are energetically expensive, and teachers make an extraordinary number of decisions in any given day.
- Your brain functionality and your gut health are connected.
- Teachers are more likely to have experienced childhood abuse/neglect than people who choose non-helping careers. This means we're at risk of accidentally harming our students interpersonally.

Strategies

- Prevent decision fatigue by routinizing as much of your life as possible.
- Eat as many different types of plant fiber as possible as routinely as possible to support a diverse gut microbiome (which, in turn, supports healthy brain functioning).
- Prioritize sleep hygiene: keep consistent sleep and wake times, protect your bed for only sleep and sex, keep devices out of the bedroom, minimize exposure to "blue" screen light during the day, and stay away from screens at least an hour before bed, and consider keeping screened devices out of your bedroom altogether.
- Consider therapy. You deserve support.

Chapter 11

Your Classroom, Your Self

In which we bring your extreme self-care into your classroom to support you, your practice, and your students.

"Discipline makes things easier."
— Dead Prez —

Stay Connected to Your Rational Brain

You have done some incredible work so far. You've figured out who and how you want to be in your classroom, and you've set up your year, your self-care, and your out-of-school life to support that vision.

Even with all of this essential work, your classroom may still feel as hectic, disorienting, anxiety-producing, and as draining as it did before you reclaimed your self-care. That's not because you're doing anything wrong. It's because classrooms are astonishingly complex situations. By attending to your classroom the way you have attended to other parts of life, you bring those eight Cs you've been cultivating (creativity, courage, curiosity, connection, compassion, clarity, calm, and confidence) into your classroom.

By building a classroom environment in which you can stay regulated, you're committing to be more available to your students. By building a classroom environment that connects to your prefrontal cortex, you ensure your ability to be present and pleasant with your students. When you're more tuned in, you can more easily make in-the-moment adjustments that would seem out of reach or overwhelming when dysregulated.

Your experience within your living, breathing, dynamic-as-all-get-out classroom is as essential as your students'. Attend to yourself as intentionally as you do a well-planned lesson. In fact, by writing yourself into the day's plans, you'll be more able to keep your prefrontal cortex online.

Stay Connected by Routinizing Predictable Disconnections

Remember how you're making thousands of decisions per day? There's a significant number of those you won't be able to anticipate. They're decisions about how to angle your shoulders so that a student feels welcomed but not pressured, if you should quickly swap two arguing partners or slow down to discuss their disagreement, if you should scrap the next activity because the class is getting so much out of the current one. If we accept that we're bad at decision making when we're overwhelmed by decision fatigue, our task becomes to remain vigilant in minimizing our in-class decision making *before* instruction begins.

One teacher I worked with simultaneously protected his decision-making and positively rewrote his relationship with a student just by putting a sign on the wall. His school culture was steeped in an adversarial stance toward students. As students are sensitive to those dynamics, it was no wonder that, early in the school year, this student had a habit of loudly wondering across the room, "Hey, Mr. Teach! When does this class get out?" To this educator's credit, he understood how this could turn into a power struggle the first time he engaged with it. Of course, we want to get students any information that will help them feel oriented and participatory in the room. We also want to minimize interruption for them and the whole class. And, it's possible the student wasn't just asking because they wondered but also because it's their developmental job to push boundaries. Aware of that developmental reality, the teacher posted bell schedules on all four walls. The next time the student asked what time class ended, the teacher smiled at him, nodded towards the posted schedule, and kept helping the student he was helping. The asking student, once invited to the developmental stage of himself that could take responsibility for knowing when class ends, nodded and refocused on his work. And didn't ask again.

When pre-deciding for instructional planning, it's helpful to think about examples like the one above; what parts of a functional classroom are students likely to have questions about, and how can I clearly and consistently answer those questions ahead of time so that we spend minimal instructional time addressing them? The more of this thinking you can do ahead of time, the more you've already decided what happens ahead of time, so you don't need to devote any additional brain power in the moment. Many behavior-modification-oriented classroom management approaches advise similarly. Unfortunately, they're all vulnerable to the same adversarial, deficit orientation thinking our structurally oppressive culture supports, so consider a heavy dose of the eight Cs when pre-choosing. We can pre-choose to dismiss or honor students. Even better, we can pre-choose to trust students and encourage them to develop the kind of behavior you hope they will. We do this by explicitly, firmly, and pleasantly pointing them back in the right direction of that behavior should they ever veer.

Routines Protect Against Bias

When we've decided ahead of time, we don't have to decide on the fly. Our on-the-fly decisions tend to be weaker and more biased.

Inconsistent policy enforcement is structural oppression's playground. For example, if MkKayla is five minutes late to first period, dominant culture has pre-programmed me to subconsciously consider that her dad has a fancy job with the district and that maybe her being five minutes late isn't that big of a deal because she's a "pretty good student." When Tyrone walks in the same five minutes late, he may be subject to me wondering whether his mom ran out of gas again or if he just "felt like" walking in late. Because we can't change our inherent biases, the minute I allow myself to launch into such biased rationalization is precisely when I allow the worst parts of dominant culture to dominate my decision making.[76] By deciding ahead of time that anything from one second after the bell to ten minutes after the bell counts as a tardy, I can simply mark them both tardy because they are both tardy. I don't have to concern myself with interpreting intention nor circumstance. I can stay available for facilitating the whole class as I need to, and stay available for more individual problem solving with either student privately later on.

Here are some (but not all) of the things you can decide before-hand:

- **Tardiness**
  - How tardy is tardy? If it's anywhere between a millisecond after the bell and ten minutes into class, communicate that explicitly.
  - How will students know a tardy has been recorded?
  - From the students' perspective, what is the incentive to be on time?

---

[76] Banaji, M. R., & Greenwald, A. G. (2016). *Blindspot: Hidden biases of good people*. Bantam.

Note: An incentive needs to be positive; students already have to manage enough guilt and shame by simply existing.

- **Absences**
  - What types of assignments can be made up?
  - What assignments require substitution activities (because they can't be replicated outside of class)?
  - How do you want students to tell you they'll be absent?
  - How do students figure out what work they missed, ideally without needing to ask you or other students about it (at least to find the thing)?
  - How do students submit make-up work? What is the absolute final deadline?

- **Bathroom Visits**
  - Do you want or need to contract around bathroom breaks? If so, how many visits per unit of time is a fair and reasonable number for an average student to need?
  - How long do you consider a bathroom break? Who tracks that?
  - What is the reward for students who don't utilize their breaks? This isn't a penalty for those who may have conditions that necessitate breaks; it's a grade-separate incentive to stay in class.

- **"Take a Minute" Procedures**
  - What may students do when they feel overwhelmed or dysregulated?
  - How would you support students to resolve interpersonal conflict?

- **Classroom Logistics**
  - Where do students pick up materials? Ideally, you can find a place in the room where you can put stacks of handouts and materials ahead of time so that you're not spending class time physically handing things around.
  - Where do backpacks and bags go?
  - Consider your safety, their comfort, and distraction minimization.
  - Where do students turn in assignments? A consistent spot is great. A set-up with multiple clearly labeled drawers may help you to keep assignments and classes organized without having to sort them in between learning episodes and passing periods.
  - How will you return graded assignments? Folder systems work well!

Particularly if you're engaging in self and peer evaluation, many grades won't be a surprise. Once you've entered the grade, you can return students' work to their folder, which lives in class. You'll know it's there, they can reference it any time, and the likelihood of misplacement is lowered.

- What's the role of phones in your classroom? As with all policies, and as I learned the hard way, make sure your administrators will support you in enforcing your approach; families seem particularly sensitive to policy enforcement around phones.

- **Classroom Culture**
  - What opportunities will you build in to "notice" students? How will you keep track of who you notice, and ensure that every-body gets noticed regularly? It may be sufficient for you to stand at the door and greet everyone. Other classes may benefit from more intentional noticing. To manage this, you can write a couple of sticky notes to celebrate something students did well (a remoralizing practice to close your day), then hand them out quietly and subtly during the next day's instruction. This lets you track who you've gotten a note to throughout the week, the term, and the year.
  - How will you support students to greet each other when class starts?
  - How will students know how you want it to sound when they discuss academic ideas? This may be lesson-by-lesson sentence frames or permanent "say something" cards on students' desks.
  - What should students do if they have a question?
  - How and when, specifically, will you teach and practice each of the above policies and expectations?

Routinize Centering Students and Relationships

Beyond in-the-moment stressors that threaten our presence and pleasantness in the classroom, some basic structural teaching realities challenge our ability to keep our prefrontal cortex in the room. All of us continue to age while our students stay the same age (assuming we're teaching the same grade level). Some of us teach the same group the same content multiple times per day. These two realities can combine to numb us to our students' experiences; our own boredom may engender our cognitive distancing as we rebuild class-room norms for the fourth, 14th, or 28th time. Meanwhile as we age, our lived experience and organic, culturally overlapping experiences are growing less and less aligned with our students'. If we don't acknowledge these components, we're setting ourselves up to over-simplify our students as stereotypes of young people. We may even stereotype ourselves as old people incapable of connection with youngsters. When we do this, we risk missing our students' unique humanities, the places where we earnestly connect.

A colleague of mine had several sticky notes posted in inconspicuous places around her classroom. They read "TAOEYO." Thinking this was some mystical mantra, I asked her about it. It is an acronym that stands for "They are only eleven years old." Wisely, my colleague had identified a reminder she could offer herself to both be compassionate to the parts of her that sometimes found boredom and frustration in answering the same questions, reviewing the same policies, and setting up the same expectations year after year while still showing up as pleasant and present to the students, who were each experiencing her class for the first time. Build in reminders that help you connect with your most aligned self while you're in your space, just as you build in ways to connect with your students themselves.

Routinizing ways to visit with learn about students (in ways where they have autonomy over what and how much they share, and we are neither voyeuristic nor trauma-mining) is a key component of staying connected during class. This can be as quick, simple, and goofy as letting students teach a move to start a 30-second dance party, or as involved as quarterly, page-long letters that students write and you respond to (using prompts to support their metacognition, explore their own values and interests, and putting zero pressure on them to be anything other than who they are).

You're Okay, They're Okay

I once coached a first-year teacher struggling to connect with his students. Out of habit, I stated that, after socioeconomic status, a student's perceived relationship with the teacher is the best predictor of student success in the classroom. Upon my saying this, this poor educator turned bright red and became visibly upset. He was never the cool kid, he explained. He was good at school because he wasn't good at people. Under the freak-out was an understandable fear; what if students didn't want a relationship with *him*?

You don't have to worry about this. When we say "relationships are important," we mean a specific type of relationship. We do not mean that you are besties. Ideally, students will like you, but that's not as important as students experiencing you as a safe, reliable, predictable person who is perpetually ready to learn about who they are in the moment. There many reasons that students might not like you; reminding them of another authority figure, representing a system that has hurt them... All of that is actually ok. You only need to worry about how you regard them.

Prioritizing earnest curiosity about your students over your insecurity increases your availability for your students.

Because you're in a mentoring role of positional power, it would be inappropriate for you to have a two-way relationship with your students. Ideally, you don't need their fondness, approval, or attention for any reason (see "Consider Therapy" in Chapter 10). All you need to do is be consistent, predictable, transparent, and unflinchingly validating about who your students are as growing humans. That is what it means to prioritize student relationships as an excellent educator.

Stay Connected to Your Body

Even if you've done a great job caring for yourself outside of class and routinizing class procedures to maximize connected instruction during class, you still have a body.

As a social animal, you are an expert at collecting and processing social cues. While this data supports you to make responsive, attentive instructional decisions, it also releases stress hormones. We release stress hormones even if everything is going great, even if we're enjoying ourselves. Being a person with other people is biologically stressful, and your body will respond like it has been built to do, even though modernity exposes us to way, way, way more interactions than our tribal, nomadic ancestors ever encountered. We have to manage our in-the-moment stress proactively.

Routinize connecting to and caring for your body in your classroom the same way you've routinized potential interruptions during class and with the same care and attention you've used to build robust self-care outside of the classroom. Notice when you're stoically bearing something that doesn't require it, and commit to addressing it for yourself.

- **Eat Food**
  - What snacks can you have on hand that are tidy, quick, nutritious, and satiating? Calendar when you'll stock up on said snacks.
  - How can you plan to manage the predictable cravings for carbs, fats, salt, and eating-for-sensation cravings that inevitably dominate a brain experiencing stress?

- **Drink Water**
  - Water is essential for basic brain functioning. Drinking it is non-negotiable. We'll address peeing in its own section. Commit to drinking water and knowing how much you drink per day.
  - You'll drink more water if it tastes good. If your building's pipes are old, invest in a filtering pitcher to refill easily from the closest faucet. Consider peppermint oil or water-flavoring syrups if that will support you to be excited about drinking more water.
  - Love your water bottle—get yourself a water bottle that makes you happy. Carry your water bottle with you, as you're more likely to use it.

- **Breathe**
  - Diaphragmatic breathing (where you take breaths deep enough that your belly expands, and your diaphragm muscle touches the top of your stomach organ) can instantly and significantly decrease the amount and type of stress hormones in your bloodstream.[77]
  - Plan out your breathing routine: When will you take three deep breaths before, during, and after your school day?
  - What additional reminders can you build in? Something like, "Every time the bell rings, I'll take a deep breath."
  - Routinize deep breaths so much that they become your automatic response in a student interaction in which you don't know what to do, or risk reacting from a state of increased stress.

Staying Connected to Your Worth—Go Pee!

Educators are known for developing "bladders of steel," putting off urination for absurd amounts of time. It's lesser known that educators develop behavioral incontinence at higher rates than the rest of the

---

[77] Ma, X., Yue, Z. Q., Gong, Z. Q., Zhang, H., Duan, N. Y., Shi, Y. T., ... & Li, Y. F. (2017). The effect of diaphragmatic breathing on attention, negative affect and stress in healthy adults. Frontiers in Psychology, 8, 874.

population.[78] While this may initially strike us as both funny and sad, I hope to move us to indignation. The factoid of our collective incontinence is a bizarre, but somehow perfect, illustration of the embodiment of BD&E.

We might limit what we take in or tightly control what we let out, metaphorically speaking, but that self-denial catches up with us at some point. Our persons remain deeply harmed when we don't insist on being human in our work. And humans have to pee.

Consider peeing as your banner of emancipation. How would your practice change with the simple, gentle, firm assertion that you will pee when you need to pee? All of a sudden, you'll need to consider building a classroom that is self-sufficient enough that you can trust your trustworthy students to keep acting like good people while you're out of the room. If that's not an option for you, that's okay. This is also a great opportunity to connect with colleagues and build a plan for who can relieve who (no pun intended) so that you each can step away for a restroom break.

Use a stopwatch to time how much time is required to pee. When there are no students in the building, start your stopwatch. Calmly, without rushing, walk to the nearest restroom, pee, wash your hands thoroughly, and return to your classroom with the same leisurely stride. When you're back, stop the stopwatch. Write down how long it took to the second, and note this information where it's easily accessible during the school day. You'll need to decide within seconds if you can squeeze in a bathroom sprint before the bell rings. This becomes easier if you know how much time a bathroom break requires.

If you drink enough water to support your brain to function optimally, your urine should be clear and copious.[79] That said, you can be smart about your water intake based on what you know about your day. It may make sense to drink a full eight-ounce glass on waking and another on exiting your shower, as you know you'll have a chance to pee before students arrive and between first and second periods. If your morning is packed, maybe just one

[78] Von Gontard, A., De Jong, T. P., Badawi, J. K., O'Connell, K. A., Hanna-Mitchell, A. T., Nieuwhof-Leppink, A., & Cardozo, L. (2017). Psychological and physical environmental factors in the development of incontinence in adults and children. Journal of Wound, Ostomy and Continence Nursing, 44(2), 181-187.

[79] Perrier, E. T. (2017). Shifting focus: From hydration for performance to hydration for health. Annals of Nutrition and Metabolism, 70(Suppl. 1), 4-12.

glass upon waking makes sense, but you can drink half of a liter over your lunch break because you have a teachers' aide in the room in the afternoons.

Like all of this work you have done, you are the expert in your context. You've rejected harmful cultural expectations about the aims of your work as well as damaging ideas about how your work is allowed to monopolize your time, relationships, and physical health. So, too, can you reject the assumption that educators just aren't as lucky as other professionals who, generally, get to pee whenever they need to. Your humanity belongs in your classroom. The status of your bladder is no exception. You matter, your humanity matters, and your body matters, and if you need to pee, pee.

Too Long; Didn't Read
Chapter 11:
Your Classroom, Your Self

Ideas
- Routinize your classroom in an intentional way that supports you to stay connected to your values, your students, your body, and your worth.

Strategies
- Build seamless solutions for any student need that could interrupt instruction (particularly in policies around tardiness, absences, making up missed work, etc.).
- Surround yourself with supportive messages and structures to help you enact your values.
- Build specific times and cues into your day to stay fed, hydrated, to breathe deeply, and to pee.

Chapter 12

Hope for the Best, Plan for Real Life

In which we acknowledge that we can only control what we can control, and if things don't go exactly how we expected, it doesn't mean we have failed. It means we are more likely to be able to find success through improvisation.

"To be fully alive, fully human, and completely awake is to be continually thrown out of the nest."

— Pema Chödrön —

Plan to Cultivate Playful Mastery

You've almost finished this whole book about how planning—particularly planning with extreme intentionality—can improve your life. Thinking that planning will make your life better is guaranteed to cause additional suffering if anyone interprets that said plans will then unfold effortlessly and precisely as intended. In fact, it's the opposite; even if you plan impeccably, your plans will never live in the world precisely as you envisioned.

The distance between plan and actuality can either be a contributing factor of burnout or a feature that fortifies against demoralization. It depends on your perspective and how you manage your expectations.

It's soothing when we see a school year neatly mapped out with the scope, sequence, objectives, evaluations, and gorgeous breaks we've protected for ourselves. And then we walk into the door of the place. "Soothing" has never described public education settings.

Things. Will. Happen. Buses will break down. Traffic will keep being a thing. The lunchroom will flood, and everyone will need to eat lunch in classrooms. The tech will fail. You will get sick. The fire drill will be missing from the school's calendar. You will get sick. There will be an assembly schedule to mourn a community member. A school board member will pop in for a photo op and offer five minutes of unsolicited advice mid-lesson. You will get sick. A child will vomit in your classroom or on you. You will get sick. A parent will have feelings that require you to attend three meetings and create four new assignments. You will forget the toothpicks, and the activity won't make sense without them.

If you fill the space between the plan and the actually-unfolding reality with stories about "what should have happened," you're filling it with vitriol that you, and you alone, will need to sort through to find a practical next step. I'm not saying it's easy to forget your beautiful plan and switch gears— I am saying that switching gears is essential.

Planning well won't guarantee that things will go according to plan.

If you can approach the experience that unfolds where your plan crosses from future tense to present tense with the eight Cs (creativity, courage, curiosity, a sense of connection, compassion, clarity, calm, and confidence), then you'll be on your way to cultivating playful mastery. You'll be able to move through most of those disruptions with your sanity intact. The differences between your plans and your actualities won't halt you, as you won't need to document every slightly-different-than-the-plan moment with indignation for the universe and everybody to notice. If you can think about your plan as a river instead of a railroad track, you'll be much more able to lean into the inevitable waves.

Why Even Plan, Then?

If things will never go according to plan, why did we waste this whole book celebrating planning? Easy. Your plan is useful even when foiled.

Though we've been discussing your plan as a product for most of the book, you've been engaging in planning as an essential process. Examining who you are, what you need, who your students are, what your system is, and how you'll need to be realistic about linking all of it together—these are all requisite thought exercises which, having completed them, set you up to be deeply responsive in the moment.

I am not recommending that you script out every second of your year before the first bell rings (heartbreakingly, if that's your bag, there are way too many school districts already on the scripted curriculum bus—I'm not inviting us to board that one).[80] Nor am I encouraging you to stop planning entirely because nothing ever works. Rather, I'm asking you to consider that planning well serves us well even when our plans fall through.

Just as learning is a process, planning is a process.

By engaging in the planning process, you're more equipped for the inevitable upheavals, no matter how far your actual lessons veer from your original plan. Because you've already made tough decisions about curriculum themes, order, and ideas to emphasize due to your planning process, you'll know (often without any additional investment) what to shift, change, or jettison amidst an unexpected real-life difference. Because you've built in frequent, authentic opportunities to connect with your students, when a student has a rough day or makes a bummer choice, you can now respond in a manner that earnestly utilizes the relationship as a lever for restorative processing. You might be able to occasionally skip some of your intentional self-care and honestly be okay. Or, you might need a whole lot more intentional self-care. But you wouldn't know unless you'd already been tuned in to how you're doing and what you need because of your planning process.

Good teachers are good at improvisation. Good teachers who are also good planners are better at improvisation. Great teachers are experts at improvisation precisely because they are disciplined planners, and disciplined planners are more likely to plan to stay.

Shall You Use Your Time?

Jack London had some strong opinions when it came to using sick or personal days: "The function of man is to live, not to exist. I shall not waste my days trying to prolong them. I shall use my time."[81]

You may or may not have administrators who will allow you to be this bold and expressive with your contracted time "off"—whether for sick or

---

[80] Timberlake, M. T., Thomas, A. B., & Barrett, B. (2017). The allure of simplicity: Scripted curricula and equity. Teaching and Teacher Education, 67, 46-52.
Fitz, J. A., & Nikolaidis, A. C. (2020). A democratic critique of scripted curriculum. Journal of Curriculum Studies, 52(2), 195-213.

[81] Shepard, I. (Ed.). (1956). Jack London's Tales of Adventure. Doubleday.

personal days. That's okay. There are many rigidly enforced cultural expectations around PTO and how it's used. Sensitivity to cultural expectations is more useful than enforcing your own unbending stance.

I was once jealous of a colleague whose mentor's first question for her was, "How are you going to use your personal days to take care of yourself?" My jealousy, however, was short-lived. Soon, I saw how no amount of personal days could counteract the school's cultural expectation that a standard educator's work week is 70 hours.

Similarly, I've worked with a principal who kept track of which teachers had used sick days. He carried this info around in a small notebook in his pocket. He didn't note tasks to follow through on or observations about instruction, students, or anything else a principal might be concerned with. But man—he knew who had used a sick day. In that school, anyone taking a sick day was at risk of illegal retribution; the number of sick days one took was the number of times per quarter he would punitively "check in on" an educator. If it could be avoided, it was best not to use sick days at that school.

Taking a hard-and-fast stance against the culture of the school can be unsafe. Taking care of yourself does not mean digging your heels in about any singular position that will misalign you with a school's culture. Culture is real, impactful, and worth considering, particularly when it comes to easily-documented HR issues. Workplace culture only shifts when both accountability and support also increase. If the history of American public education is any indicator, don't hold your breath. It's okay to be sensitive to the situation, read the room, and play these precious days the way that is truly best for you—at home, at work, and in your heart.

Substitutes: Can't Live With 'Em, Can't Find 'Em

You'll need to miss class.

You won't want to. You'll drag your carcass to school, contagious as a yawn, to avoid missing the day. If needing a sub is inevitable, you'll put off making the final call until the last minute because you dread it so much. Anyone who has needed a substitute knows that nothing can turn your classroom into a *Lord of the Flies* reenactment faster. And yet here we are; you're human, and your students are human. The whole teaching-learning thing is a deeply human enterprise, and humans fail each other.

You'll fail your students by needing a minute (not actually a failure—untwist your knickers—all the other stuff we've said so far is still valid). Your sub will fail to facilitate class the way you'd imagined, particularly if you expect them to pick up where you left off, because subbing is a poorly-supported gig. Finally, your kids will fail because the temptation is too great; the urges to assert their power and to move their bodies will overtake them as their loyalty to you starts to seep out of the room the moment you're not in it. This is inevitable. Unless you plan for it.

I was lucky to be placed with Mrs. Laurie Turner at Fremont Union High School for my student teaching. I could not have been trained by a more exceptional educator. Unfortunately, Laurie fell ill that year, and I ended up stepping in for a significant period of time (thank goodness, everything with her health worked out okay). Within the first week of me as instructor of record and 42ish students in 2nd period, I encountered a test. The bathroom was occupied during passing period.

By the time we got mid-way through a second 90-minute block, I was afraid my bladder would actually explode. I stuck my head outside the door as a colleague of Laurie's passed by during his prep period and asked if he would watch my class while I ran to the restroom. He peeked in at the class, looked at me, said "Get over yourself, would you?" and walked away. That turned out to be the most instructive thing an incidental mentor said to me.

You didn't anticipate a paragraph connecting why having a substitute rarely goes well, pee breaks, and structural oppression, did you? It's like this; one of the features of White supremacy culture we haven't addressed much is the "I'm the only one" idea. If "I'm the only one," I'll accidentally build students' dependency on me. I'll accidentally motivate them to care about my opinion through either respect and love or fear and threat. If, however, I think that students are innately capable of rich, meaningful learning, and they are supported to self-monitor and own that learning, then the importance of the specific facilitator at any given moment becomes less critical. Writ large, this shift has powerful implications for students and their learning. On a smaller scale, I'm more likely to be able to pee when I need to, and substitutes are likely to merely rock the boat (instead of capsizing).

It matters that there is an adult in the room. Students will always be members of a hierarchical, social species, and so, no matter how autonomous and collectively motivated they are, will always be sensitive to the presence of an adult in the room. To support the social jolt that a leadership transition can have, consider desensitizing that transition by practicing. Grab a colleague (whom you trust with your students) ideally from across the hall and, one or two times per week, swap classes for a few minutes. Do so with as much or as little notice for your students as you want, then reflect on anything that came up afterwards. Make this part metacognitive, and weave in some social, emotional, and spiritual self-care principles. Let students reflect on who they want to be in the classroom and why, regardless of who is in the room. Even if you never need a sub the whole year (that is not a dare), the process will still encourage self-determination and minimize your students' social reactivity.

Ideally, you can build a "room watching" agreement with a trusted colleague. Even more ideally, you can both be compensated whenever you need to cover each other's classes in each other's absence. To make this happen, explore your district's policy regarding holding a substitute credential, and encourage your colleagues to do the same. This way, you can get paid when you cover for each other. In the frustrating and annoyingly common circumstance that you need a sub but can't get one, all of the effort described in the previous paragraph will be even more worth it.

To prepare for a sub that isn't available, you can think of it like being your own sub. Bring back a repeatable, skills-based lesson format that your students can practice while you're feeling good and carry out with less intervention when you're not doing so great. This works better if this is interactive and structural instead of something like "read a chapter and answer the questions at the end." This approach pays off twofold; when you should be home sick but you're forced to teach due to a lack of subs, you will have prepped your students for when your best self isn't leading the room. Practicing what to do with your class so that they know what to do with other adults in the room, rather than building yourself in as the lead in a cult of personality, may save their day and yours even when you're around.

For example, if students know how to write an introduction paragraph and revise with a partner using three articles provided, then you can use that format and that protocol again and again for different combinations of articles. If students know how to pair (partner up), share (describe their processes and answers to each other), compare (list similarities and differences in approaches and answers), care (name one thing they appreciated about their partner's approach) and square (decide together about the approaches they think will best lead to a correct answer), their mathematics worksheet, then they know it. They're ready to support each other in engaged, meaningful learning structures even if you, at some point, need to "facilitate" this process with your head on a table, technically facing the class with your eyes open as you wait for the Dayquil to kick in.

Plan For Catastrophe

Things will happen that Dayquil cannot fix. Plan for it. If your school doesn't already force you to make emergency sub plans at the start of the year, do it anyway. It's okay to have a total check-the-box plan, likely involving a movie.

Once you're a few weeks into the year, it's also okay to adjust that emergency plan to better suit your students and your needs. It's nice to build sub plans around skills and activity structures that are iterative or that build on themselves throughout the year. For example, if your students engage in reading circles, have a reading circle sub plan ready to go. No matter where they are in the year, your students will be ready to participate in some way, particularly if you modify the reading circle structure (which they would already be familiar with) with readings that you include in the plans, ensuring that a forgotten novel here or there wouldn't impact any student's experience of the activity.

It's tempting to think that we won't have to use our sub plans because we don't want to. Unfortunately, that's a great way to set up those plans to fail. Instead of thinking of sub days as wasted, consider how you can incentivize engagement. By saving special content that is slightly outside of what you normally may include but interesting to your students, you can override their sub-affected hesitation with their own excitement.

I got to work with a middle school teacher whose particular gift was in learning about and honoring students' interests. That year diamonds were a particularly hot symbol in hip-hop new releases, and so he built an entire unit around them. When this teacher wrote sub plans in the fashion we're exploring, he may have included an article about a hop-hop artist's involvement in supporting conflict-free lab-grown diamonds. It would be okay for the unit if it that lesson was never utilized because he never needed a sub, but it was exciting and additive enough for students that it would have been useful if it was necessary.

Build ready-to-rock catastrophe plans. Print out enough copies for all students. If your plan requires multiple handouts, staple them together in packets so that everyone has everything they need with one handing-out event. Place them all in a bright folder or envelope labeled "emergency sub plans" or similar. Take a photo of where you keep that stuff in the room and email that photo and location description to your admin, department or team leader, and colleague across the hall.

Way, way, way too often, we don't take days off when we need them because preparing you for a substitute takes more energy than just going in. If you put in some energy before you're experiencing something that would initiate needing a day away from school, it will feel much less stressful, and may even take less energy.

Be Ready for Next Week

While it's true that your whole-year plan doesn't need to be at the lesson-plan level, it's also true that planning for tomorrow tonight is a fast track to burnout. Once per week, protect time to plan for the coming week. Know which products you need to make, calendar when you're going to make them, and do it all in a way that guarantees that the products, and not just the plans, are done days before you need them.

Like your broad-strokes planning, your lesson-by-lesson plan will likely change slightly as the lesson approaches. That's okay. Your planning won't be wasted. When we're under stress, it's easier to tweak the wording in already-authored instructions than to invent instructions from scratch. Building products a week before you use them also allows you to do so under so much less stress that your brain will function better, and you'll be more productive in less time.

On hearing this advice, some may argue that it won't work for them because they thrive on pushing up to the deadline. This can true for many people, often for a range of reasons. For a very slim few, procrastination and last-minute product creation do help them to produce better products. For those whose procrastination is motivated by perfectionism (oh, hi, White Supremacy Culture!), the reward of procrastination is relief from the pressures of perfection; if they had more time, it would have been the ideal they had held in their mind for the last month, and that's why it's not perfect, see? Some procrastinate because they are overwhelmed by their inability to predict the future accurately; something might change, so why do anything? For those whose procrastination is about a paralyzing fear of failure, the longer we put it off, the more torturous it is to even consider starting a task. Because most teacher prep happens in collegiate academic settings which are far more predictable than a public school setting, procrastination seems to have been rewarded because, well, y'all graduated, after all. Now may be the time to consider that the cost of your procrastination might outweigh the benefits.

You do not need the added stress of waiting in line behind six colleagues two minutes before the first bell because you made your handouts at 6:17 a.m. You don't need the extra cortisol surge, let alone to torpedo that perfect activity because you used your prep period to sprint to the grocery store nearest your school to discover they were out of food coloring. You don't need the extra anxiety of realizing you made the jigsaw groups wrong because you fell asleep twice last night while trying to complete it.

Teaching is stressful enough. If you're going to dodge BD&E, you'll do it by minimizing all unnecessary stress. Self-inflicted stress in the name of procrastination, for any reason, is self-harming. Put in the significant work required at the start of the year to start one week ahead and maintain space, time, and task planning to allow yourself to stay one week ahead for the entire term. Allowing our Inner Child to put things off and then tormenting ourselves with Inner Parent admonishment is as predictable of a cycle as it is a harmful one. Investing in what you want most over what you want in the moment by preparing well is the sort of Inner Adult-motivated self-care that supports your present self to love on your future self.

We Do Not Learn From Experience

According to American constructivist John Dewey, "We do not learn from experience, we learn from reflecting on experience."[82] If you've internalized nothing else from this book, let's hope you've accepted that our intentions mean nothing if we don't protect sufficient time to enact them. If we want to build a reflective teaching practice, one that integrates the inevitable learning and growing available to us each and every day, we have to plan time to reflect.

I thought I was so clever as a first-year teacher. I kept a pad of sticky notes next to my calendar on my desk. If I noticed something I didn't like about a lesson, if I had a correction for a worksheet, if I had a brilliant idea for a modification to better differentiate an activity, I would jot it down on a sticky note and place it... somewhere. Usually, either on the calendar itself or on a copy of the handout I wanted to change, but sometimes on the whiteboard, my desk, or my pocket if I was rushing around (pockets are not the optimal application surfaces for sticky note technology, it turns out). The week before I started my second year in the classroom, I discovered the flaw in my clever plan. As I flipped through materials, I found sticky note after sticky note. My mid-class scribblings were barely decipherable, both in handwriting and cognitive coherence. They did a great job documenting my dissatisfaction from the previous year. They did not help me fix it.

My lessons, products, and student-facing materials started improving when I started protecting regular, designated time to reflect upon them. The started improving drastically when I also protected the time to integrate that reflection into the actual products, themselves.

Build Your Own Predictability

You can minimize your decision-making load, enforce your routines, and ensure that you complete critical tasks by routinizing your routines (whoa).

When there are two thousand things to do, and you have 45 minutes in which you desperately want to be productive, you are subject to an increased likelihood of eating chips and "looking up articles" (i.e., social media abyss-plunging) instead of actually accomplishing any one of the two thousand

---

[82] Dewey, J. (1997). How we think. Dover Publications. (Original work published 1910)

things. You can prevent decision fatigue during times you need to be productive. By mapping your "free" time, you can ensure that you'll know what to focus on.

It can look something like this:

Weekday	Prep Period Tasks	After School Tasks
Mon.	Plan next week List things to make and materials to get	Enter today's peer-graded work Set up room for tomorrow morning
Tues.	Prep next week's presentations	Enter today's peer-graded work Set up room for tomorrow morning Prep student work for tomorrow's PLC
Wed.	Prep next week's handouts	Enter today's peer-graded work Set up room for tomorrow morning Print required materials for next week
Thurs.	Write specific feedback on peer-graded assignments	Enter today's peer-graded work Set up room for tomorrow morning Shop for materials for next week
Fri.	Reflect on week, make changes Alter handouts and activities	Make five positive phone calls home

You can and should modify this general plan to fit your life. If you take your kids to gymnastics on Thursdays via a stressful and unpredictable commute, and it brings you joy to watch them practice for a few quiet moments, don't make that the day you plan to shop for materials. If watching your kids at gymnastics is boring for you (don't worry, no judgment), or you just need to be as efficient as possible, maybe running to the store while they're tumbling is perfect.

The better you know and are honest with yourself about who you are and what you need, the more you'll be able to outline a general weekly task plan to ensure that critical components are addressed regularly. It's possible (even likely) that you won't be able to get everything done during your planning period. That's okay. Simply anticipating the time, acknowledging that using it well will be at least 45 minutes less you'll need to do that night, and relieving yourself of the decision of how to spend that time (having already committed to using it well) will increase your efficiency and efficacy.

Go Slow to Go Fast

You did it. You did it! You realized that you are essential enough, important enough, and valuable enough to value yourself in your essential and important work in the classroom—at least enough to consider reading this book. Then you explored a ton of ideas, and even more concrete strategies and suggestions to help you care for yourself and your students towards enduring learning and increased capacity and connected humanity in your classroom. The list of ideas and strategies is not short.

You do not have to do everything at once.

Start with one thing. Perhaps this year, setting up your calendar to support yourself is "first step" enough on the planning side, and exploring peer grading is enough as you implement liberating approaches in your classroom. That's great! This book will still be around next year, and you can work in other ideas and strategies then.

If you know the lay of the land and are ready to more assertively implement new ideas, consider focusing on one idea until it's integrated, or focus on one idea per week. You could list what you want to implement, and in what order, or flip to a page like an extreme self-care tarot deck and pick an idea from whichever page you open. The only wrong way to implement new strategies would be in any manner that makes you feel more overwhelmed.

The version of you that's interested in "planning to stay" is the version of you that you, your family, your friends, and your students deserve. It's also the version that stands the best chance of enjoying a sane and satisfying career inside the classroom and a rich, full life outside of it.

Too Long; Didn't Read
Chapter 12:
Hope for the Best, Plan for Real Life

Ideas

- Planning to stay takes time and practice. Be gentle with yourself as you get better at it and as things inevitably go differently than you had planned.
- Even when things unfold differently than planned, having planned well empowers us to be better at adjusting.
- The impact of substitutes can be minimized by making student behavior with subs metacognitive, and by routinizing activities that a sub might facilitate.
- Using your sick and personal days can be liberating, but it doesn't mean if you don't use them, you're not liberated. School culture influences this decision.

Strategies

- Invest in 100% turn-key high-quality sub plans (copies already made, instructions already written, presentations already built and saved on a memory stick in the same place as the rest of the materials).
- Use class structures to keep student experience and expectations cohesive.
- Practice swapping classrooms with other teachers, even if it's just for a few minutes, and use those opportunities to coach students about your expectations when they're supervised by someone other than you.
- Stay one week ahead in your lesson planning and materials collection whenever humanly possible.
- Plan time to reflect (per unit or per quarter) and physically modify any changes you'd like to make in your lessons at that time.
- Predictably disperse predictable tasks throughout your week so that they don't stack up and so that nothing gets too far out of balance if an emergency comes up (example on p. 181).
- You don't need to change everything at once. Start with one thing to change first, do it until it becomes a habit, then add another. When you're ready, add another. And another.

Afterword

For most of us, school was a set-up, a dirty rotten lie about how the world works. We were told one of two general storylines. One version said that if we follow the syllabus, write the papers, and complete the word problems, if we accept that there are correct answers and arrive at them, we would earn recognition and validation. We would be good. This story caused harm in convincing us that controlling our actions will control outcomes. Experiencing the perceived power to control outcomes was a privilege which didn't continue once we entered into "the real world." But not everyone experienced their own schooling as free and fair. The second storyline told us that school was a dirty rotten lie for the opposite reason. No matter how hard we tried, nothing we did was right. We were bad. Our world happened to us without rules of causality or fairness. Our actions did not lead to predictable impacts, so we stopped trying. The harm this version caused was to dis-connect us from agency to impact our own lives through our actions.

Like most truths, the truth here is somewhere in the middle. We can't control everything. But that doesn't mean we are powerless.

Instead of it being a bummer that life is unfair, what if it's a relief? What if you are freed to focus on the things you can impact? Focusing solely on the things we can control sounds so... nice! It also sounds tough because habit change is tough. At first, changing our habitual world view requires significant focus and energy. Once learned and integrated, however, getting good at focusing on what we *can* control can be downright liberating.

If you have tried everything, read this book, tried more of everything, and still find teaching untenable, it's okay. You're okay. Healing requires time, space, and permission. Give yourself permission to take the time and space you need. Consider that you've completed a tour of duty. If you come back after you take a break, great! If you don't come back, also great! While you may leave the classroom, there are still ways you can participate.

If you need to leave the classroom, consider utilizing the skills you've built towards becoming a committed, strategic advocate for getting public educators the support, respect, and resources the profession deserves. Your letters to the editor, monthly commentary at school board meetings, and positive relationship building with local legislators as an expert who can support necessary policy reform are all essential contributions that your still-in-the-classroom colleagues can't prioritize. If you can't plan to stay, you can certainly plan to stay engaged.

If you are planning to stay, now might be a good time to answer the question, "Stay where, exactly?" Planning to stay doesn't necessarily mean you commit to a particular physical classroom, school, district, or even state. You're an educator; you're flexible. Perhaps this is an invitation to hold your educator identity with the same fluidity that you do a new activity you're trying out. Decide which values, opportunities, collegial relationships, and potential career paths will allow you to plan to stay. Define and commit to a set of requisite conditions and guiding principles. If and when something in your professional context inevitably changes, having already considered the bare minimum you need may support you to feel less like you have to stay in a situation that doesn't work for you. Your commitment to stay is bolstered by your commitment to extreme self-care; your commitment to extreme self-care will always mediate your commitment to stay.

The work suggested in these pages has an ongoing nature. My own work is also ongoing. My work to support educators from outside of the classroom continues to emerge, as does my own personal work to manage the tendencies that continue to push me towards burnout, demoralization, and exploitation. When the first edition of this book came out, I was encouraged to promise that I would be there to support you every step of the way, that I would provide an ever-renewing suite of resources and perpetual availability to make whatever products or trainings anyone needed. Caving to this contract was symptomatic and enabling. It built me in to your energizing, remoralizing, and boundary-building practice as if you couldn't do that work yourself, while simultaneously setting me up to martyr myself to your salvation in an unsustainable promise.

As I continue build my own boundaried, energizing, values-aligned practice, I am continually confronted with how little I am capable of "accomplishing." As someone who previously identified with achievement as indicated by the number of products produced and/or published or the number of workshops held, I have had to reckon with the formidable distance between where my unhealthy bar used to be set and where my realistic benchmarks are these days. I am still surprised when I look back on what I used to be capable of "accomplishing." It feels good to be so much more connected to my own life, my own relationships, my own work these days. And I continue to work with my own Inner Parent, whose favorite hobby remains reminding me of my own insufficiency.

Not only am I physically incapable of supporting every individual educator engaging in anti-BD&E work, but my Inner Adult reminds be that doing so would be counter-productive. This work is like any other work in growth and transformation. We may be able to do it surrounded by supportive community, but at the end of the day, we have to walk the metaphorical path with our own bodies. We have to do the work for ourselves. Just as I believe in students as trustworthy, motivated learners, I believe that you know what you need, and that you'll figure out what work you need to do and you'll do it. I don't need to continue to participate in your process in order for you to progress. You've got this.

And, I anticipate I'll continue in the work moving forward. If I write, design, or facilitate in the future, I can promise that I will do so from a foundation of reciprocity. I will only offer what I can give without resentment, without fueling BD&E culture, including within my own life. I hope that this stance can free you from any lingering sense that anyone outside of you can rescue you. I hope that it can support you to fully engage in your own healing adventure.

As I imagine you allowing yourself to loosen your grip on all of that stuff for which you feel accountable but that you can't control, I'm imagining that stress evaporating from your shoulders in a fine mist and drifting into the atmosphere. As you allow for the increasing possibility that you have agency over your time, your relationships, and your experiences, I imagine a gentle smile permeating you so fully that it gently loosens your intercostal muscles and allows your diaphragm to relax into deeper, calmer breaths. Sitting here imagining how your relationship to your own pleasure, your own power, your own sense of how much you matter might impact you, other people start coming into view.

As I see the tens and hundreds of students who you will support with your practice, I tear up a bit, heartened in knowing that they got to experience at least one teacher like you. Panning out further, I can see you being quietly, gently, supportively surrounded by the hundreds and thousands of educators who are doing this same nourishing work for themselves.

You've already imagined how it would feel to be in a classroom as you do this work. Now imagine what it would be like to be in a school where each classroom was led by an educator who was planning to stay in this way. Imagine administrators whose sole roles were to support you in planning to stay connected to what matters most for students as growing humans. Dare to envision a district, a school board, even a state legislature full of people dedicated to schools as energizing, just, and humanizing places. Such a shift could be possible. And every shift starts somewhere.

You matter. Your work matters. And how you matter within your work matters. The work of planning to stay is individual work, for sure. But it isn't selfish. And you're not alone.

We can stay in touch via www.jesscleeves.com, where I'll post info about workshops, planners, other books, etc.

I can't wait to hear where your work takes you as you plan to stay.

Acknowledgements

I'm indebted to my family, particularly my mom, dad, and sister, for their patience during the times I disappeared into typing, or, more disconcerting, thinking.

To the good humans at University Neighborhood Partners, particularly Julianne Rabb, Lenn Rodriguez, Paul Kuttner, and Jennifer Meyer-Glenn, for sharing space and vision to support teachers. Thank you, Dr. Jordan Gerton and Mary Burbank, and the University of Utah's College of Education, for legitimizing this deep, integrated work by offering my time and offering teachers academic credit for their efforts.

Tyler Asman and Allison Antwi, thank you for showing me how to invest in visionary solutions, including my own capacity. Nikole Hannah-Jones, it was timely to learn from your wisdom in choosing those who choose you.

To the classroom teachers who took time away from their already over-burdened lives to support this work, particularly Abby Barry (middle/ high school reading), Danielle Johnson (elementary special education), Molly Michaels (early childhood special education), and Robert Violano (middle school science), thank you, thank you, thank you.

To Anna Hansen at The Hex Press, for all of the icons, images, and iterations, your humanity adds as much humanity to these pages as your skill.

To the thinkers, writers, and visionaries whose work shapes mine, but who I didn't quote directly in this particular book, I'm indebted to you. Gratitude, particularly, to adrienne maree brown, Dee Brown, Linda Darling-Hammond, Dr. Dave Derezotes, Paulo Freire, Ibram X. Kendi, Robin Wall Kimmerer, Bettina Love, Charles C. Mann, Heather McGhee, Mary Rose O'Reilly, Richard Rothstein, Ronald Takaki, Linda Thai, and Laura van Dernoot Lipsky.

All remaining gratitude goes to my love, who resolutely soothed every bout of insecurity and kept bringing me tea without me needing to ask for it. Your unwavering support surprises, delights, and inspires me.

About the Author

Jess Cleeves is an educator obsessed with relationships. Before becoming a classroom teacher, she worked with learners in informal contexts (after-school programs for first through third graders, outdoor programming for adjudicated students, etc). After earning her MAT in secondary science education at Stanford's Teacher Prep program (STEP), Jess taught in underserved communities in California, Colorado, and Utah, supporting all ages and stages of students from middle school through experienced in-service educators and graduate students. Jess earned a second Master's of Social Work at the University of Utah while she served as the Associate Director for Equitable Instruction and Clinical Support at the Center for Science and Mathematics Education.

In her current work as a licensed clinical social worker, Jess supports people, organizations, and communities to heal, liberate, and connect. Combining her original training as a conservation biologist, her 20-year career as a science educator, and her commitment to critical social work, Jess facilitates individual and couples' therapy and workshops (often geared towards educators), coaching for administrators, training for schools and organizations, and community organizing. Particularly important in Jess' work: helping people be in relationship with themselves and their kin (both human and non-human), getting quickly to the heart of issues towards enacting solutions, and identifying and addressing the ways systemic oppression operates and impacts all of us.

Connect with Jess at www.jesscleeves.com